잉글리쉬 마이갓으로
내신 영어 1등급

베이직	플러스	풀버전
단어	객관식 변형 (4회)	베이직
원문 + 해석	주관식 변형 (4회)	플러스
빈칸/순서/선택 (4회)	**8회독**	**17회독**
객관식 변형 (2회)		
주관식 변형 (3회)		
9회독		

변형 문제 더 보기

Composition | 플러스

01 문장 의미 추론

최상위권을 위한
밑줄 친 문장과 의미가 같은 문장을
객관식 선지에서 고르는 문제입니다.

선지를 통해 유사 표현과
반대 표현을 함께 익힙니다.

02 요약문 어휘 위치

전체 요약문을 파악한 뒤,
지정된 위치에 가장 자연스럽게 들어갈
단어를 찾는 문제입니다.

내신과 수능에서 요구하는
핵심 정보 요약력을 기를 수 있습니다.

03 주제 문장 선택

글 전체의 중심 생각을
표현한 영어 문장을 찾는 문제입니다.

영어로 주제와 세부 정보의 관계를
이해하는 능력을 키웁니다.

04 빈칸 문장 선택

문장의 흐름과 논리를 바탕으로,
빈칸에 가장 자연스럽게 들어갈 문장을
고르는 문제입니다.

연결력과 독해력을
함께 점검할 수 있습니다.

05 Paraphrase

지문 속 핵심 내용을
파생어와 동의어 중심으로 정리하며,
다양한 표현에 대한
이해력을 높이는 문제입니다.

06 주제문 완성

박스 속 보기를 활용해 주제문을
완성하는 문제입니다.

문장의 **연결 논리와 핵심 내용을 파악**하
는 능력을 키워줍니다.

07 요약문 빈칸 완성

실제 시험에서 자주 출제되는
요약 + 어휘형 문제를 한 세트로 묶어
마무리 점검에 도움을 줍니다.

08 요약문 SET

2지 선다와 빈칸 유형을 연달아 풀며
요약문을 만드는 세트 문제입니다.

상위권을 가르는 고난이도 대비에
효과적입니다.

마
이
Plus
갓

2025년 고2 모의고사

WORK BOOK

6月

2025 고2 6월 모의고사 내신대비용 WorkBook & 변형문제

2025 고2 6월 모의고사

❶ Plus 1　　**❷ Plus 2**　　**❸ Plus 3**　　**❹ Plus 4**　　**❺ Plus 5**　　**❻ Plus 6**　　**❼ Plus 7**　　**❽ Plus 8**

18

1) 지문에서 밑줄 친 *"reflect on your contributions"* 가 의미하는 바로 가장 적절한 것은?

Dear Ms. Lopez,
We want to express our gratitude for your dedication as a Spanish instructor. With exceptional teaching skills, you have significantly improved our students' progress and confidence in Spanish. As the year is about to end, it is time for us to *reflect on your contributions* and consider the renewal of your contract. Given your positive impact, we would like to offer an extension of your contract for the next academic year. We believe
your continued involvement will further enhance our students' learning experience and academic achievement. We look forward to your response.
Sincerely,
James Martin
Principal

① measure your attendance record
② think carefully about the value of your work
③ evaluate your students' test results only
④ compare your performance with other teachers
⑤ discuss your contract terms in detail

19

2) 지문에서 밑줄 친 *"a wave of calm wash over him"*가 의미하는 바로 가장 적절한 것은?

Peter stepped out of the freezing night air and into the brightly lit hospital lobby, holding his three-year-old daughter in his arms. The harsh light made her look even more unwell, her face all red and sweaty. Her fever had started suddenly, just before dinner, but it wouldn't go down despite his efforts. At the front desk, he explained her symptoms, his concern growing with every moment. They were quickly led to the doctor, who reassured him and carefully examined his daughter. After the doctor gave her a shot, her fever went down and she seemed more comfortable. As Peter watched her sleep peacefully that night, he felt *a wave of calm wash over him*.

① he suddenly became tired after the stressful night
② he felt unsure about the doctor's treatment
③ he experienced a strong feeling of relief
④ he wanted to stay awake to watch over his daughter
⑤ he remembered similar situations from his own childhood

20

³⁾ 지문에서 밑줄 친 *"build walls around themselves"*가 의미하는 바로 가장 적절한 것은?

Imagine you have the best tea in the world and you put it into a bag that's impermeable. It won't work. You just won't be able to make a cup of tea. For the teabag to work, it needs to be porous. You need the tea and the water to come in contact with each other. In our lives too, we cannot survive and thrive in isolation. Leaders need to be careful not to *build walls around themselves* that prevent people from reaching out to them. As a leader, you need to be able to touch other people. The tea was meant to mix with the water. Similarly all of us were designed to work with other people, with teams, and with society at large.

① offer guidance to their team members actively
② create clear personal and professional goals for team members
③ improve their skills without distraction by themselves
④ focus only on achieving measurable success
⑤ isolate themselves and limit communication with others

21

⁴⁾ 지문에서 밑줄 친 *"a horizon of his own"* 가 의미하는 바로 가장 적절한 것은?

It is difficult, if not impossible, to define the limits which reason should impose on the desire for wealth; for there is no absolute or definite amount of wealth which will satisfy a man. The amount is always relative, that is to say, just so much as will maintain the proportion between what he wants and what he gets; for to measure a man's happiness only by what he gets, and not also by what he expects to get, is as pointless as to try and express a fraction which shall have a numerator but no denominator. A man never feels the loss of things which it never occurs to him to ask for; he is just as happy without them; whilst another, who may have a hundred times as much, feels miserable because he has not got the one thing he wants. In fact, every man has *a horizon of his own,* and he will expect as much as he thinks it is possible for him to get.

① a personal limit to his desires and expectations
② an exact calculation of his total wealth
③ a strong connection to his cultural background
④ an ability to achieve financial independence
⑤ a tendency to compare himself with others

22

5) 지문에서 밑줄 친 *"the language of smell"*가 의미하는 바로 가장 적절한 것은?

All of the restaurants are using carefully chosen words to evoke vivid mental images of delicious food and rich desserts in order to draw the potential customer to their particular establishment. Just like the restaurants, nature has its own dining establishments. In a fashion similar to the restaurants' financial dependence upon drawing in many customers, the restaurateurs of the natural world (i.e., flowers) must also attract potential diners to sample their offerings. In the natural world, there are no neon signs or flashy words in which to market a potential meal to hungry animals. These restaurants that I am referring to are the world's flowers, and the potential guests are the host of organisms that visit flowers to obtain nectar and other valuable resources. Instead of using a written language or neon sign, they advertise their offerings just as effectively using *the language of smell*.

① a symbolic message conveyed through color patterns
② a set of chemical signals used to warn predators
③ an instinctive behavior triggered by physical contact
④ a means of communication using scents to attract visitors
⑤ a genetic adaptation that prevents cross-species feeding

23

6) 지문에서 밑줄 친 *"emotional interest rate"*가 의미하는 바로 가장 적절한 것은?

Would you rather receive $1,000 in a year or $1,100 in a year and a month? Most people will opt for the larger sum in thirteen months — where else will you find a monthly interest rate of 10 percent. A wise choice, since the interest will compensate you generously for any risks you face by waiting the extra few weeks. Second question: Would you prefer $1,000 today cash on the table or $1,100 in a month? If you think like most people, you'll take the $1,000 right away. This is amazing. In both cases, if you hold out for just a month longer, you get $100 more. In the first case, it's simple enough. You figure: "I've already waited twelve months; what's one more?" Not in the second case. The introduction of "now" causes us to make inconsistent decisions. Science calls this phenomenon *hyperbolic discounting*. The closer a reward is, the higher our *"emotional interest rate"* rises and the more we are willing to give up in exchange for it.

① the rate at which market conditions affect investment returns
② the increased value people place on immediate rewards
③ the financial cost of delaying gratification
④ the logical calculation used to compare different offers
⑤ the predicted inflation rate over a given time period

24

7) 지문에서 밑줄 친 *"it is actually determined"*가 의미하는 바로 가장 적절한 것은?

Of central importance for understanding the development of handedness is the answer to the question of when in development *it is actually determined* whether a child will be left-handed or right-handed. It was long thought that handedness could only be reliably determined in elementary school, when a child learns to write. However, this assumption is incorrect. In fact, scientific studies show that left-handedness is established in many children long before elementary school — interestingly, even before birth in most people. In such studies, the hand and arm movements of unborn children in the womb are recorded using ultrasound images. Using this technique, it was shown that a clear preference for the movement of the right arm exists as early as 10 weeks after fertilization. In this study, ultrasound images of 72 unborn children 10 weeks after fertilization were evaluated and 85% showed more movements of the right arm than the left. This number is already very close to the approximately 89.4% right-handers among adults.

① it is gradually taught through repetitive training from early childhood
② it depends mainly on cultural influences regardless of genetic aspects
③ it is completely random throughout life despite hard training
④ it is openly expressed through language since elementary school
⑤ it is biologically established at a specific point in development

25

8) 지문에서 밑줄 친 *"the reverse was true"*가 의미하는 바로 가장 적절한 것은?

The graph above shows US dairy product imports in selected countries from 2018 to 2020. Among the four countries above, Mexico consistently recorded the highest imports of US dairy products from 2018 to 2020. However, US dairy product imports in Mexico decreased from 2019 to 2020, while *the reverse was true* in the other three countries during the same period. In Indonesia, US dairy product imports in 2020 were more than twice those in 2018. The increase in US dairy product imports in the Philippines from 2018 to 2019 was smaller than that in Indonesia in the same period. China was the only country where imports of US dairy products dropped between 2018 and 2019.

① imports stayed at the same level
② imports fluctuated unpredictably
③ imports increased instead of decreased
④ imports decreased more rapidly than expected
⑤ imports were unaffected by market trends

26

9) 지문에서 밑줄 친 "*strengthened his reputation*"가 의미하는 바로 가장 적절한 것은?

Filippo Brunelleschi is considered to be the founding father of Renaissance architecture. He was born in Florence in 1377. Filippo was artistically talented, and trained as a goldsmith and a clockmaker before becoming an architect. When he was around 25, he traveled to Rome with his friend, the sculptor Donatello, where he studied the remains of ancient Roman buildings. His first architectural commission was the Ospedale degli Innocenti, which is one of the great Renaissance buildings. A number of other fine works, including chapels in Florentine churches, *strengthened his reputation*. And the stunning dome of Il Duomo is his masterpiece. He also designed machinery to produce special effects in theatrical productions. He died in Florence and was buried in Il Duomo.

① gave him more opportunities to travel abroad
② enhanced how highly he was regarded by others
③ forced him to change his architectural style
④ caused disagreements with fellow architects
⑤ limited his ability to work in other fields

29

10) 지문에서 밑줄 친 "*stick with it*"가 의미하는 바로 가장 적절한 것은?

In art, there are a number of ways to use perspective to obtain the illusion of depth, including using colors and graduated values of black and white, and accurately drawing the subject by applying the rules of the geometric system of perspective. In order to achieve perspective, you must make a number of observations. The forms or objects that you draw on a flat surface actually have depth and dimension in real life. As you view them and place their shapes and forms on a drawing surface, try to represent that depth to make the objects appear realistic and three-dimensional. Objects appear differently when viewed from various positions. Because of this, it's important to establish the viewpoint, and *stick with it*. When observing a subject, you see depth and three dimensions. When you draw this subject onto a flat surface as it appears to the eye, you are drawing in perspective.

① examine the object from multiple angles
② change the position to capture better details
③ adjust the viewpoint frequently during the process
④ maintain a consistent point of observation
⑤ follow the geometric rules very strictly

30

11) 지문에서 밑줄 친 "*this notion*"가 의미하는 바로 가장 적절한 것은?

Low oil prices are a good thing, because it means lower energy costs of production for the majority of industries, not least the automobile and the logistics industries. Firms directly benefit from the decrease in their costs of production and provision of services. This has the effect of stimulating the aggregate supply and provides a stimulus for growth. Conversely, a sudden rise in oil prices due to a shrink in oil production is never good news, even though it definitely gives a big boost to the energy sector. A look through the history of oil price fluctuations verifies *this notion*, as this has been the subject of much economic research. Following an oil price jump of 10 per cent due to a contraction in supply, an economy (as typified by the US economy) typically sees its output (GDP) slowed by close to 1 percentage point. For a $15 trillion economy, that is a loss of $150 billion in potential wealth or economic growth. Conversely, there has never been much concern with oil price decreases following an excess in its supply.

① the idea that a rise in oil prices negatively affects the economy
② the belief that oil price changes are difficult to predict
③ the assumption that oil prices have no long-term impact
④ the claim that energy sector growth benefits all industries
⑤ the opinion that oil production levels should remain constant

31

12) 지문에서 밑줄 친 "*wakes up the self*"가 의미하는 바로 가장 적절한 것은?

We might forget an anecdote about a stranger because it makes few connections with our existing associations, but we won't forget a piece of gossip about our cousin. There's one complex network that is larger and quicker to access than all others — the self. We've been thinking about ourselves in our whole lives. (In fact, there were entire years during junior high when we weren't capable of thinking about much else.) So if a new piece of information has something to do with *us*, it will be more easily and thoroughly processed. It hits even closer to home than our actual home — we can take a vacation away from our home, but not from *ourselves*. The most effective communicators find ways to make the abstract personal. Consider the warning that law schools give to motivate first-year law students concerning the rigors of their program. Hearing that "the first-year dropout rate is 33%" is an abstract statistic. "Look to your left, look to your right. One of the three of you won't be joining us next fall" *wakes up the self*.

① encourages students to form study groups personally
② reminds students to be more punctual collectively
③ helps students focus on campus life thoroughly
④ urges students to seek professional advice actively
⑤ makes students personally relate to the information

32

13) 지문에서 밑줄 친 "*win over the masses*"가 의미하는 바로 가장 적절한 것은?

Steve Jobs used analogy to get people to embrace the new technology. Before computers, people worked in a physical world. We used paper and pens and physical file folders and so on. The idea of working in a virtual world was radically different. Or at least *seemed* radically different. What Jobs understood was that a physical office was fundamentally similar to a virtual office. To *win over the masses*, Jobs drew strong analogies between the traditional workplace people knew well with the new, unfamiliar virtual workplace. In the pre-computer workplace, when ideas were written on paper it was called . . . a document. When those documents needed to be stored they were put in . . . a folder. And those folders were kept on . . . a desk. Documents, folders, and desktops are the terms we use in our virtual work because Steve Jobs understood that using familiar terms would make the new technology easier to understand. The parallels between the physical and virtual workplace now seem obvious.

① persuade experts to adopt the technology
② create competition among leading companies
③ gain the acceptance of ordinary people
④ avoid criticism from skeptical users
⑤ increase government support for innovation

33

14) 지문에서 밑줄 친 "*being blinded by modern lights*"가 의미하는 바로 가장 적절한 것은?

Turtle hatchlings have, it seems, evolved to crawl toward the light. For millions of years this was a highly rational and effective strategy because the light on a dark beach represented the reflection of the moon and stars on the water's surface. Following the lights led baby turtles back home to the sea. The problems started when humans began building beachfront homes and sparkling hotels on the other side of the beach. Now after hatching, turtles heading for the brightest nearby lights were being guided straight into traffic. Are self-destructive sea turtles naturally irrational? Yes, in the modern world. But there's a deeper truth. Turtles are basing their decisions on simple cues that were perfectly rational for their ancestors; these days, however, their evolved decision-making mechanisms are *being blinded by modern lights*.

① adapting quickly to new sources of food
② instinctively avoiding unfamiliar surroundings
③ learning to rely on human guidance
④ having their natural behavior disrupted by artificial factors
⑤ increasing their sensitivity to light over time

34

15) 지문에서 밑줄 친 "*this concept*"가 의미하는 바로 가장 적절한 것은?

Sensory organs are the only channels of communication between the brain and the outside world. Simply put, the brain is not designed to sense on its own. For instance, an exposed brain would neither sense light shining on it nor feel something touching it. In fact, patients are often kept awake during brain surgery, which can help a surgeon isolate specific regions of the brain. The ancient Greek philosopher Aristotle recognized this characteristic of the brain over 2,000 years ago when he said, "Nothing is in the mind that does not pass through the senses." *This concept* can be seen clearly when volunteers are blind-folded and placed in the warm water of a sensory deprivation tank. They soon experience visual, auditory, and tactile (touch) hallucinations, as well as incoherent thought patterns. From these experiments and others, it is apparent that we need constant input from our senses to carry out functions that give us personality and intellect.

① the brain can control bodily functions without effort
② sensory deprivation has long-term health effects
③ hallucinations are caused by warm water environments
④ the brain can store unlimited amounts of information
⑤ all knowledge must enter the mind through the senses

35

16) 지문에서 밑줄 친 "*hardwired*"가 의미하는 바로 가장 적절한 것은?

The writer and zoologist Desmond Morris observed that our feet communicate exactly what we think and feel more honestly than any other part of our bodies. Why are the feet and legs such accurate reflectors of our sentiments? For millions of years, long before humans spoke, our legs and feet reacted to environmental threats (e.g., hot sand, ill-tempered lions) instantaneously, without the need for conscious thought. Our limbic brains made sure that our feet and legs reacted as needed by either ceasing motion, running away, or kicking at a potential threat. This survival regimen, retained from our ancestral heritage, has served us well and continues to do so today. In fact, these age-old reactions are still so *hardwired* in us that when we are presented with something dangerous or even disagreeable, our feet and legs still react as they did in prehistoric times.

① firmly programmed into our natural behavior
② easily influenced by social expectations
③ gradually weakened through conscious training
④ quickly adapted to changing environments
⑤ mostly controlled by external rewards

36

17) 지문에서 밑줄 친 "*won out*"가 의미하는 바로 가장 적절한 것은?

The transition from an oral culture, in which knowledge was handed down through stories, songs, and apprenticeships, to a literate one, based on the written word, was held back for centuries by the lack of suitable writing material. Stone and clay tablets were used, but they were prone to fracture and were bulky and heavy to transport. Wood suffers from splitting and is susceptible to decay. Wall paintings are static and space is limited. The invention of paper, said to be one of the four great inventions of the Chinese, solved these problems, but it wasn't until the Romans replaced the scroll with the codex — or, as we call it now, the book — that the material reached its full potential. That was two thousand years ago, and it is still a dominant form of the written word. That paper, a much softer material than either stone or wood, *won out* as the guardian of the written word is a remarkable materials story.

① was replaced by newer materials quickly
② was preserved only in certain regions
③ became the preferred and most successful option
④ was modified to suit modern technologies
⑤ was stored mainly for historical interest

37

18) 지문에서 밑줄 친 "*working through the connections*"가 의미하는 바로 가장 적절한 것은?

A reason for a conclusion is very unlikely to consist in a single claim. No matter how we might state it in short-hand, it is, analytically, a complex interaction of many ideas and implications. The reason must be broken down into a chain of more precise premises. For example, the claim that 'university education should be free for all Australians' might be supported by the reason that 'the economy benefits from a well-educated Australian population'. But is our analysis of the situation clearly expressed in just one statement? Hardly. The conclusion is about universities and free education, while the reason introduces some new ideas: economic benefit and a well-educated population. While the link between these two ideas and the conclusion might seem obvious, the purpose of reasoning is to avoid assuming the 'obvious' by carefully *working through the connections* between the various ideas in the initial statement of our reason.

① identifying the emotional appeal behind a claim
② carefully analyzing how different ideas relate to each other
③ rephrasing the argument to make it sound more convincing
④ adding new evidence to support unrelated claims
⑤ simplifying the reasoning to make it easier to remember

38

19) 지문에서 밑줄 친 "*selective of persons*"가 의미하는 바로 가장 적절한 것은?

The word "migration" is almost always reported in the popular media and even in scientific literature as a problem or a crisis. For example, migrants are assumed to overcrowd cities, clog up labor markets, and increase poverty. The other questionable assumption is that most migration is involuntary — people fleeing natural or man-made disasters. The reality, however, is more complex, and many migrants are simply seeking greater economic opportunity. Of course migration can and does create social and economic problems. But migration can also be a solution for many preexisting problems. For example, out-migration generally redistributes workers from places of labor surplus to areas where there is greater demand or more opportunity. Migration is generally *selective of persons* who are younger, healthier, more flexible, and more willing to endure hardship in hopes of a better life relative to their prospects in their places of origin. Most research that examines long-term outcomes of migration, including remittances and intergenerational mobility, finds positive "long-term" effects on places of origin and destination.

① discouraging older generations from migrating collectively
② allowing only highly educated people to migrate
③ encouraging families to migrate together simultaneously
④ increasing restrictions on migration policies
⑤ involving mainly people with certain advantageous traits

39

20) 지문에서 밑줄 친 "*depriving governments of the power*"가 의미하는 바로 가장 적절한 것은?

The big problem with money created by the government is that those who run the government always face the temptation to create more money and spend it. Whether among ancient kings or modern politicians, this has happened again and again over the centuries, leading to inflation and the many economic and social problems that follow from inflation. For this reason, many countries have preferred using gold, silver, or some other material that is inherently limited in supply, as money. It is a way of *depriving governments of the power* to expand the money supply to inflationary levels. Gold has long been considered ideal for this purpose, since the supply of gold in the world usually cannot be increased rapidly. When paper money is convertible into gold whenever the individual chooses to do so, then the money is said to be "backed up" by gold. This expression is misleading only if we imagine that the value of the gold is somehow transferred to the paper money, when in fact the real point is that the gold simply limits the amount of paper money that can be issued.

① giving governments full control over interest rates
② preventing governments from controlling the value of gold
③ limiting governments' ability to print excessive money
④ encouraging governments to promote international trade
⑤ allowing governments to collect more taxes from citizens

40

21) 지문에서 밑줄 친 "*This contradicts the assumptions*"가 의미하는 바로 가장 적절한 것은?

The study of emotions and decision making is now of considerable importance. This involves the application of various tools afforded by neuroscience. One important stream of the literature examines people with brain damage and how damage to particular parts of the brain known to be responsible for particular cognitive functions impacts on decision making. One example of this research is the work of Antonio Damasio, who finds that when the emotional part of the brain is damaged, this actually reduces the efficacy of decision making. Good decisions are a product of the emotional part of the brain working in conjunction with the deliberative part. *This contradicts the assumptions* of conventional economics, where emotions play a negative role in the decision−making process. Here it is assumed that decision making can be modeled as being generated in a stoic, unemotional fashion, and that's why decisions tend to be optimal. But the evidence suggests that emotions actually play an important and, often, a positive role in decision making.

① The finding that emotional brain damage impairs decision making directly challenges the economic view that emotions only interfere with rational choices.
② The belief that emotions and logic work best in isolation is widely supported by both economic theory and neuroscience.
③ Conventional economists have long maintained that emotional responses are essential for achieving optimal decision outcomes.
④ Scientific evidence confirms that eliminating emotion from decision making improves accuracy and leads to better results.
⑤ Research in neuroscience has consistently reinforced the idea that emotions are dangerous distractions from logical thinking.

41~42

22) 지문에서 밑줄 친 "*tyranny of choice*"가 의미하는 바로 가장 적절한 것은?

Shoppers confronted with the choice of thirty different varieties of gourmet chocolates are more likely to walk away without buying any, compared with when they are presented with only half a dozen choices. If employees are given a free trip to Paris, they are happy. If you give them a free trip to Hawaii, they are happy. But if you offer them the choice between the two destinations, they are less happy, no matter what they choose. Why might choice be so disruptive? The reason is that choice forces us to make comparisons and acknowledge relative disadvantages. People who choose Paris complain that it doesn't have the ocean and those who choose Hawaii regret that it doesn't have the museums. Psychologist Barry Schwartz calls this the '*tyranny of choice*' because rather than providing freedom, it actually constrains our decision−making. He argues that wider choice increases unhappiness because we worry that we are going to make the wrong decision and so we get stressed about trying to process all the comparisons in an effort to get it right. This both increases our fear of making the wrong choice and raises expectations that we should be able to get the best choice. Having made the choice, we
then start to regret, wondering whether it was the right one.

① a situation where options are limited by external forces
② a method of motivating people to choose freely through increased rewards
③ a system in which only experts can make decisions correctly
④ a condition where having too many options makes decision−making harder
⑤ a process where all available choices lead to the same result

43~45

23) 지문에서 밑줄 친 "*feeling the urgency of the situation*"가 의미하는 바로 가장 적절한 것은?

As the train pulled into a quiet countryside station, the gentle chatter of passengers filled the air. Linda was excited to finally visit her grandparents after two years. She watched people getting onto the train and hurriedly finding their seats. A moment later, an elderly woman struggled with a heavy bag, trying to sit down next to her. The bag seemed almost too big for her small body. Linda hesitated, unsure if the elderly woman would want her help. But soon, she chose to assist the woman. "Let me help you with your bag," she said. Before she could reach the bag, the elderly woman suddenly lost her balance and fell down. She lay on her back, and her face was pale. Linda froze for a moment, *feeling the urgency of the situation*. She quickly knelt down beside the fallen

woman, as a few people rushed over. Linda carefully tapped the elderly woman's shoulder to check if she was alright. The woman groaned softly, trying to gather her strength. Linda moved closer, sliding a hand under the woman's back. As the woman's eyes slowly opened, she reassured her softly, "It's okay, just relax for a moment." Linda helped the woman sit up slowly, then guided her back to her seat. As the situation settled, people around went back to their seats. As the elderly woman finally calmed down, she looked at Linda with a smile. "I'm so sorry," she said. "I have low blood pressure, and the sudden movement of the train must have made me feel dizzy. Thank you so much for helping me." Linda nodded gently in response, then turned her gaze back to the peaceful countryside scene. She thought that no matter how unsure she might feel, even the smallest act of help is much better for someone in need than doing nothing.

① realizing that immediate action was needed
② worrying about how other passengers would react
③ deciding to wait for a professional to arrive
④ noticing that the train had suddenly stopped
⑤ regretting not helping with the bag earlier

2025 고2 6월 모의고사

❶ Plus 1　　❷ Plus 2　　❸ Plus 3　　❹ Plus 4　　❺ Plus 5　　❻ Plus 6　　❼ Plus 7　　❽ Plus 8

18

1) 보기의 순서를 바르게 맞추어 요약문을 작성하였을 때, 요약문의 세 번째 부분에 오는 것을 고르시오.

Dear Ms. Lopez,
We want to express our gratitude for your dedication as a Spanish instructor. With exceptional teaching skills, you have significantly improved our students' progress and confidence in Spanish. As the year is about to end, it is time for us to reflect on your contributions and consider the renewal of your contract. Given your positive impact, we would like to offer an extension of your contract for the next academic year. We believe your continued involvement will further enhance our students' learning experience and academic achievement. We look forward to your response.
Sincerely,
James Martin
Principal

① improved students'
② contract renewal is
③ offered for next year
④ exceptional teaching
⑤ Spanish skills, so

19

2) 보기의 순서를 바르게 맞추어 요약문을 작성하였을 때, 요약문의 세 번째 부분에 오는 것을 고르시오.

Peter stepped out of the freezing night air and into the brightly lit hospital lobby, holding his three-year-old daughter in his arms. The harsh light made her look even more unwell, her face all red and sweaty. Her fever had started suddenly, just before dinner, but it wouldn't go down despite his efforts. At the front desk, he explained her symptoms, his concern growing with every moment. They were quickly led to the doctor, who reassured him and carefully examined his daughter. After the doctor gave her a shot, her fever went down and she seemed more comfortable. As Peter watched her sleep peacefully that night, he felt a wave of calm wash over him.

① a sudden fever, got
② Peter's daughter had
③ the hospital, and
④ treated at
⑤ recovered by night

20

3) 보기의 순서를 바르게 맞추어 요약문을 작성하였을 때, 요약문의 세 번째 부분에 오는 것을 고르시오.

Imagine you have the best tea in the world and you put it into a bag that's impermeable. It won't work. You just won't be able to make a cup of tea. For the teabag to work, it needs to be porous. You need the tea and the water to come in contact with each other. In our lives too, we cannot survive and thrive in isolation. Leaders need to be careful not to build walls around themselves that prevent people from reaching out to them. As a leader, you need to be able to touch other people. The tea was meant to mix with the water. Similarly all of us were designed to work with other people, with teams, and with society at large.

① porous teabags,
② connected like
③ with people and community
④ allowing interaction
⑤ good leaders stay

21

4) 보기의 순서를 바르게 맞추어 요약문을 작성하였을 때, 요약문의 세 번째 부분에 오는 것을 고르시오.

It is difficult, if not impossible, to define the limits which reason should impose on the desire for wealth; for there is no absolute or definite amount of wealth which will satisfy a man. The amount is always relative, that is to say, just so much as will maintain the proportion between what he wants and what he gets; for to measure a man's happiness only by what he gets, and not also by what he expects to get, is as pointless as to try and express a fraction which shall have a numerator but no denominator. A man never feels the loss of things which it never occurs to him to ask for; he is just as happy without them; whilst another, who may have a hundred times as much, feels miserable because he has not got the one thing he wants. In fact, every man has a horizon of his own, and he will expect as much as he thinks it is possible for him to get.

① expectations constantly rise,
② desire for wealth
③ and unreachable
④ making satisfaction relative
⑤ is endless because

22

5) 보기의 순서를 바르게 맞추어 요약문을 작성하였을 때, 요약문의 세 번째 부분에 오는 것을 고르시오.

All of the restaurants are using carefully chosen words to evoke vivid mental images of delicious food and rich desserts in order to draw the potential customer to their particular establishment. Just like the restaurants, nature has its own dining establishments. In a fashion similar to the restaurants' financial dependence upon drawing in many customers, the restaurateurs of the natural world (i.e., flowers) must also attract potential diners to sample their offerings. In the natural world, there are no neon signs or flashy words in which to market a potential meal to hungry animals. These restaurants that I am referring to are the world's flowers, and the potential guests are the host of organisms that visit flowers to obtain nectar and other valuable resources. Instead of using a written language or neon sign, they advertise their offerings just as effectively using the language of smell.

① flowers attract
② words to advertise
③ attract customers, using
④ scents instead of
⑤ animals like restaurants

23

6) 보기의 순서를 바르게 맞추어 요약문을 작성하였을 때, 요약문의 세 번째 부분에 오는 것을 고르시오.

Would you rather receive $1,000 in a year or $1,100 in a year and a month? Most people will opt for the larger sum in thirteen months — where else will you find a monthly interest rate of 10 percent. A wise choice, since the interest will compensate you generously for any risks you face by waiting the extra few weeks. Second question: Would you prefer $1,000 today cash on the table or $1,100 in a month? If you think like most people, you'll take the $1,000 right away. This is amazing. In both cases, if you hold out for just a month longer, you get $100 more. In the first case, it's simple enough. You figure: "I've already waited twelve months; what's one more?" Not in the second case. The introduction of "now" causes us to make inconsistent decisions. Science calls this phenomenon *hyperbolic discounting*. The closer a reward is, the higher our "emotional interest rate" rises and the more we are willing to give up in exchange for it.

① immediate reward is available now
② larger delayed
③ chosen over sooner
④ ones, except when
⑤ rewards are often

24

7) 보기의 순서를 바르게 맞추어 요약문을 작성하였을 때, 요약문의 세 번째 부분에 오는 것을 고르시오.

Of central importance for understanding the development of handedness is the answer to the question of when in development it is actually determined whether a child will be
left-handed or right-handed. It was long thought that handedness could only be reliably determined in elementary school, when a child learns to write. However, this assumption is incorrect. In fact, scientific studies show that left-handedness is established in many children long before elementary school — interestingly, even before birth in most people. In such studies, the hand and arm movements of unborn children in the womb are recorded using ultrasound images. Using this technique, it was shown that a clear preference for the movement of the right arm exists as early as 10 weeks after fertilization. In this study, ultrasound images of 72 unborn children 10 weeks after fertilization were evaluated and 85% showed more movements of the right arm than the left. This number is already very close to the approximately 89.4% right-handers among adults.

① before birth, as unborn
② handedness develops
③ early preference for
④ babies show
⑤ right-hand movement

25

8) 보기의 순서를 바르게 맞추어 요약문을 작성하였을 때, 요약문의 세 번째 부분에 오는 것을 고르시오.

The graph above shows US dairy product imports in selected countries from 2018 to 2020. Among the four countries above, Mexico consistently recorded the highest imports of US dairy products from 2018 to 2020. However, US dairy product imports in Mexico decreased from 2019 to 2020, while the reverse was true in the other three countries during the same period. In Indonesia, US dairy product imports in 2020 were more than twice those in 2018. The increase in US dairy product imports in the Philippines from 2018 to 2019 was smaller than that in Indonesia in the same period. China was the only country where imports of US dairy products dropped between 2018 and 2019.

① others saw increase while
② dairy, but
③ Mexico's imports decreased
④ Mexico consistently
⑤ imported most US

26

9) 보기의 순서를 바르게 맞추어 요약문을 작성하였을 때, 요약문의 세 번째 부분에 오는 것을 고르시오.

Filippo Brunelleschi is considered to be the founding father of Renaissance architecture. He was born in Florence in 1377. Filippo was artistically talented, and trained as a goldsmith and a clockmaker before becoming an architect. When he was around 25, he traveled to Rome with his friend, the sculptor Donatello, where he studied the remains of ancient Roman buildings. His first architectural commission was the Ospedale degli Innocenti, which is one of the great Renaissance buildings. A number of other fine works, including chapels in Florentine churches, strengthened his reputation. And the stunning dome of Il Duomo is his masterpiece. He also designed machinery to produce special effects in theatrical productions. He died in Florence and was buried in Il Duomo.

① architect and
② Brunelleschi, trained
③ as goldsmith,
④ designed Florence's famous
⑤ became Renaissance

27

10) 보기의 순서를 바르게 맞추어 요약문을 작성하였을 때, 요약문의 세 번째 부분에 오는 것을 고르시오.

Youth Leaders Camp
This camp is an annual event to improve your leadership.
We look forward to meeting you soon in Canada.
Dates: July 5 – 7, 2025
Ages: 17 – 19
Place: University of Drakemont
Programs
– Day 1: Team Building & Leadership Skills Workshop
– Day 2: Culture Tour
– Day 3: Leadership Project Planning & Presentations
Participation Fee: $700
Notes
– Registration is only available online at www.ylc2025.com.
– Participation fee includes everything except for the flight tickets to Canada.
For more information, please visit our website.

① Youth Leaders Camp
② offers teens
③ workshops, tours,
④ and leadership projects
⑤ over three days in Canada

28

11) 보기의 순서를 바르게 맞추어 요약문을 작성하였을 때, 요약문의 세 번째 부분에 오는 것을 고르시오.

Jog, walk, pick up trash, and conserve the Earth!
When: September 13, 2025
Where: Lake Union
Details
– The event starts at 11:00 a.m.
– There is no participation fee.
– You'll walk and run around the lake while picking up trash.
Notes
– Wear comfortable athletic clothes and running shoes for your safety.
– Garbage bags will be provided.
– If it rains, the event will be cancelled.
If you have any questions, please email us at information@ploggingrun.org.

① encourages eco-friendly
② Union in September
③ up trash around Lake
④ Plogging event
⑤ jogging by picking

29

12) 보기의 순서를 바르게 맞추어 요약문을 작성하였을 때, 요약문의 세 번째 부분에 오는 것을 고르시오.

In art, there are a number of ways to use perspective to obtain the illusion of depth, including using colors and graduated values of black and white, and accurately drawing the subject by applying the rules of the geometric system of perspective. In order to achieve perspective, you must make a number of observations. The forms or objects that you draw on a flat surface actually have depth and dimension in real life. As you view them and place their shapes and forms on a drawing surface, try to represent that depth to make the objects appear realistic and three-dimensional. Objects appear differently when viewed from various positions. Because of this, it's important to establish the viewpoint, and stick with it. When observing a subject, you see depth and three dimensions. When you draw this subject onto a flat surface as it appears to the eye, you are drawing in perspective.

① shapes and

② To draw realistic

③ viewpoint when drawing

④ depth, artists observe

⑤ stick to a consistent

30

13) 보기의 순서를 바르게 맞추어 요약문을 작성하였을 때, 요약문의 세 번째 부분에 오는 것을 고르시오.

Low oil prices are a good thing, because it means lower energy costs of production for the majority of industries, not least the automobile and the logistics industries. Firms directly benefit from the decrease in their costs of production and provision of services. This has the effect of stimulating the aggregate supply and provides a stimulus for growth. Conversely, a sudden rise in oil prices due to a shrink in oil production is never good news, even though it definitely gives a big boost to the energy sector. A look through the history of oil price fluctuations verifies this notion, as this has been the subject of much economic research. Following an oil price jump of 10 per cent due to a contraction in supply, an economy (as typified by the US economy) typically sees its output (GDP) slowed by close to 1 percentage point. For a $15 trillion economy, that is a loss of $150 billion in potential wealth or economic growth. Conversely, there has never been much concern with oil price decreases following an excess in its supply.

① reduce production

② stimulate economy, while

③ costs and

④ price hikes shrink GDP growth

⑤ Low oil prices

31

14) 보기의 순서를 바르게 맞추어 요약문을 작성하였을 때, 요약문의 세 번째 부분에 오는 것을 고르시오.

We might forget an anecdote about a stranger because it makes few connections with our existing associations, but we won't forget a piece of gossip about our cousin. There's one complex network that is larger and quicker to access than all others — the self. We've been thinking about ourselves in our whole lives. (In fact, there were entire years during junior high when we weren't capable of thinking about much else.) So if a new piece of information has something to do with *us*, it will be more easily and thoroughly processed. It hits even closer to home than our actual home — we can take a vacation away from our home, but not from *ourselves*. The most effective communicators find ways to make the abstract personal. Consider the warning that law schools give to motivate first-year law students concerning the rigors of their program. Hearing that "the first-year dropout rate is 33%" is an abstract statistic. "Look to your left, look to your right. One of the three of you won't be joining us next fall" wakes up the self.

① we better
② to strong personal
③ remember self-related info
④ because it links
⑤ associations in the brain

32

15) 보기의 순서를 바르게 맞추어 요약문을 작성하였을 때, 요약문의 세 번째 부분에 오는 것을 고르시오.

Steve Jobs used analogy to get people to embrace the new technology. Before computers, people worked in a physical world. We used paper and pens and physical file folders and so on. The idea of working in a virtual world was radically different. Or at least *seemed* radically different. What Jobs understood was that a physical office was fundamentally similar to a virtual office. To win over the masses, Jobs drew strong analogies between the traditional workplace people knew well with the new, unfamiliar virtual workplace. In the pre-computer workplace, when ideas were written on paper it was called . . . a document. When those documents needed to be stored they were put in . . . a folder. And those folders were kept on . . . a desk. Documents, folders, and desktops are the terms we use in our virtual work because Steve Jobs understood that using familiar terms would make the new technology easier to understand. The parallels between the physical and virtual workplace now seem obvious.

① tools to virtual ones
② analogy to connect
③ for easier tech adoption.
④ Steve Jobs used
⑤ physical office

33

16) 보기의 순서를 바르게 맞추어 요약문을 작성하였을 때, 요약문의 세 번째 부분에 오는 것을 고르시오.

Turtle hatchlings have, it seems, evolved to crawl toward the light. For millions of years this was a highly rational and effective strategy because the light on a dark beach represented the reflection of the moon and stars on the water's surface. Following the lights led baby turtles back home to the sea. The problems started when humans began building beachfront homes and sparkling hotels on the other side of the beach. Now after hatching, turtles heading for the brightest nearby lights were being guided straight into traffic. Are self-destructive sea turtles naturally irrational? Yes, in the modern world. But there's a deeper truth. Turtles are basing their decisions on simple cues that were perfectly rational for their ancestors; these days, however, their evolved decision-making mechanisms are being blinded by modern lights.

① baby turtles once

② to sea, but now

③ lights leading to danger

④ follow artificial

⑤ followed moonlight

34

17) 보기의 순서를 바르게 맞추어 요약문을 작성하였을 때, 요약문의 세 번째 부분에 오는 것을 고르시오.

Sensory organs are the only channels of communication between the brain and the outside world. Simply put, the brain is not designed to sense on its own. For instance, an exposed brain would neither sense light shining on it nor feel something touching it. In fact, patients are often kept awake during brain surgery, which can help a surgeon isolate specific regions of the brain. The ancient Greek philosopher Aristotle recognized this characteristic of the brain over 2,000 years ago when he said, "Nothing is in the mind that does not pass through the senses." This concept can be seen clearly when volunteers are blind-folded and placed in the warm water of a sensory deprivation tank. They soon experience visual, auditory, and tactile (touch) hallucinations, as well as incoherent thought patterns. From these experiments and others, it is apparent that we need constant input from our senses to carry out functions that give us personality and intellect.

① brain alone cannot

② input through organs

③ awareness and thought

④ is essential for

⑤ sense because sensory

35

18) 보기의 순서를 바르게 맞추어 요약문을 작성하였을 때, 요약문의 세 번째 부분에 오는 것을 고르시오.

The writer and zoologist Desmond Morris observed that our feet communicate exactly what we think and feel more honestly than any other part of our bodies. Why are the feet and legs such accurate reflectors of our sentiments? For millions of years, long before humans spoke, our legs and feet reacted to environmental threats (e.g., hot sand, ill-tempered lions) instantaneously, without the need for conscious thought. Our limbic brains made sure that our feet and legs reacted as needed by either ceasing motion, running away, or kicking at a potential threat. This survival regimen, retained from our ancestral heritage, has served us well and continues to do so today. In fact, these age-old reactions are still so hardwired in us that when we are presented with something dangerous or even disagreeable, our feet and legs still react as they did in prehistoric times.

① instinctively, as
② modern behavior
③ feet reflect emotions
④ evolutionary responses
⑤ remain strong in

36

19) 보기의 순서를 바르게 맞추어 요약문을 작성하였을 때, 요약문의 세 번째 부분에 오는 것을 고르시오.

The transition from an oral culture, in which knowledge was handed down through stories, songs, and apprenticeships, to a literate one, based on the written word, was held back for centuries by the lack of suitable writing material. Stone and clay tablets were used, but they were prone to fracture and were bulky and heavy to transport. Wood suffers from splitting and is susceptible to decay. Wall paintings are static and space is limited. The invention of paper, said to be one of the four great inventions of the Chinese, solved these problems, but it wasn't until the Romans replaced the scroll with the codex — or, as we call it now, the book — that the material reached its full potential. That was two thousand years ago, and it is still a dominant form of the written word. That paper, a much softer material than either stone or wood, won out as the guardian of the written word is a remarkable materials story.

① paper and codex
② earlier materials
③ replacing heavy,
④ evolutionized writing,
⑤ fragile, and immobile

37

20) 보기의 순서를 바르게 맞추어 요약문을 작성하였을 때, 요약문의 세 번째 부분에 오는 것을 고르시오.

A reason for a conclusion is very unlikely to consist in a single claim. No matter how we might state it in short-hand, it is, analytically, a complex interaction of many ideas and implications. The reason must be broken down into a chain of more precise premises. For example, the claim that 'university education should be free for all Australians' might be supported by the reason that 'the economy benefits from a well-educated Australian population'. But is our analysis of the situation clearly expressed in just one statement? Hardly. The conclusion is about universities and free education, while the reason introduces some new ideas: economic benefit and a well-educated population. While the link between these two ideas and the conclusion might seem obvious, the purpose of reasoning is to avoid assuming the 'obvious' by carefully working through the connections between the various ideas in the initial statement of our reason.

① a conclusion into

② on one vague claim

③ good reasoning breaks

④ precise premises

⑤ instead of relying

38

21) 보기의 순서를 바르게 맞추어 요약문을 작성하였을 때, 요약문의 세 번째 부분에 오는 것을 고르시오.

The word "migration" is almost always reported in the popular media and even in scientific literature as a problem or a crisis. For example, migrants are assumed to overcrowd cities, clog up labor markets, and increase poverty. The other questionable assumption is that most migration is involuntary — people fleeing natural or man-made disasters. The reality, however, is more complex, and many migrants are simply seeking greater economic opportunity. Of course migration can and does create social and economic problems. But migration can also be a solution for many preexisting problems. For example, out-migration generally redistributes workers from places of labor surplus to areas where there is greater demand or more opportunity. Migration is generally selective of persons who are younger, healthier, more flexible, and more willing to endure hardship in hopes of a better life relative to their prospects in their places of origin. Most research that examines long-term outcomes of migration, including remittances and intergenerational mobility, finds positive "long-term" effects on places of origin and destination.

① migration is

② beneficial, redistributing

③ often voluntary and

④ improving opportunities

⑤ labor and

39

22) 보기의 순서를 바르게 맞추어 요약문을 작성하였을 때, 요약문의 세 번째 부분에 오는 것을 고르시오.

The big problem with money created by the government is that those who run the government always face the temptation to create more money and spend it. Whether among ancient kings or modern politicians, this has happened again and again over the centuries, leading to inflation and the many economic and social problems that follow from inflation. For this reason, many countries have preferred using gold, silver, or some other material that is inherently limited in supply, as money. It is a way of depriving governments of the power to expand the money supply to inflationary levels. Gold has long been considered ideal for this purpose, since the supply of gold in the world usually cannot be increased rapidly. When paper money is convertible into gold whenever the individual chooses to do so, then the money is said to be "backed up" by gold. This expression is misleading only if we imagine that the value of the gold is somehow transferred to the paper money, when in fact the real point is that the gold simply limits the amount of paper money that can be issued.

① can't easily overproduce
② limits inflation
③ since governments
④ a rare resource
⑤ Gold-backed money

40

23) 보기의 순서를 바르게 맞추어 요약문을 작성하였을 때, 요약문의 세 번째 부분에 오는 것을 고르시오.

The study of emotions and decision making is now of considerable importance. This involves the application of various tools afforded by neuroscience. One important stream of the literature examines people with brain damage and how damage to particular parts of the brain known to be responsible for particular cognitive functions impacts on decision making. One example of this research is the work of Antonio Damasio, who finds that when the emotional part of the brain is damaged, this actually reduces the efficacy of decision making. Good decisions are a product of the emotional part of the brain working in conjunction with the deliberative part. This contradicts the assumptions of conventional economics, where emotions play a negative role in the decision-making process. Here it is assumed that decision making can be modeled as being generated in a stoic, unemotional fashion, and that's why decisions tend to be optimal. But the evidence suggests that emotions actually play an important and, often, a positive role in decision making.

① working with reason,
② rational economic models
③ emotions help
④ challenging purely
⑤ decision making by

41~42

24) 보기의 순서를 바르게 맞추어 요약문을 작성하였을 때, 요약문의 세 번째 부분에 오는 것을 고르시오.

Shoppers confronted with the choice of thirty different varieties of gourmet chocolates are more likely to walk away without buying any, compared with when they are presented with only half a dozen choices. If employees are given a free trip to Paris, they are happy. If you give them a free trip to Hawaii, they are happy. But if you offer them the choice between the two destinations, they are less happy, no matter what they choose. Why might choice be so disruptive? The reason is that choice forces us to make comparisons and acknowledge relative disadvantages. People who choose Paris complain that it doesn't have the ocean and those who choose Hawaii regret that it doesn't have the museums. Psychologist Barry Schwartz calls this the 'tyranny of choice' because rather than providing freedom, it actually constrains our decision-making. He argues that wider choice increases unhappiness because we worry that we are going to make the wrong decision and so we get stressed about trying to process all the comparisons in an effort to get it right. This both increases our fear of making the wrong choice and raises expectations that we should be able to get the best choice. Having made the choice, we then start to regret, wondering whether it was the right one.

① increase stress and
② despite more freedom
③ people less satisfied
④ too many choices
⑤ regret, making

43~45

25) 보기의 순서를 바르게 맞추어 요약문을 작성하였을 때, 요약문의 세 번째 부분에 오는 것을 고르시오.

As the train pulled into a quiet countryside station, the gentle chatter of passengers filled the air. Linda was excited to finally visit her grandparents after two years. She watched people getting onto the train and hurriedly finding their seats. A moment later, an elderly woman struggled with a heavy bag, trying to sit down next to her. The bag seemed almost too big for her small body. Linda hesitated, unsure if the elderly woman would want her help. But soon, she chose to assist the woman. "Let me help you with your bag," she said. Before she could reach the bag, the elderly woman suddenly lost her balance and fell down. She lay on her back, and her face was pale. Linda froze for a moment, feeling the urgency of the situation. She quickly knelt down beside the fallen woman, as a few people rushed over. Linda carefully tapped the elderly woman's shoulder to check if she was alright. The woman groaned softly, trying to gather her strength. Linda moved closer, sliding a hand under the woman's back. As the woman's eyes slowly opened, she reassured her softly, "It's okay, just relax for a moment." Linda helped the woman sit up slowly, then guided her back to her seat. As the situation settled, people around went back to their seats. As the elderly woman finally calmed down, she looked at Linda with a smile. "I'm so sorry," she said. "I have low blood pressure, and the sudden movement of the train must have made me feel dizzy. Thank you so much for helping me." Linda nodded gently in response, then turned her gaze back to the peaceful countryside scene. She thought that no matter how unsure she might feel, even the smallest act of help is much better for someone in need than doing nothing.

① fainting elderly
② small actions matter
③ realizing even uncertain
④ Linda helped a
⑤ woman on train,

2025 고2 6월 모의고사

❶ Plus 1　❷ Plus 2　❸ Plus 3　❹ Plus 4　❺ Plus 5　❻ Plus 6　❼ Plus 7　❽ Plus 8

18

1) 다음 글의 주제로 가장 적절한 것을 고르시오.

Dear Ms. Lopez,
We want to express our gratitude for your dedication as a Spanish instructor. With exceptional teaching skills, you have significantly improved our students' progress and confidence in Spanish. As the year is about to end, it is time for us to reflect on your contributions and consider the renewal of your contract. Given your positive impact, we would like to offer an extension of your contract for the next academic year. We believe your continued involvement will further enhance our students' learning experience and academic achievement. We look forward to your response.
Sincerely,
James Martin
Principal

① comparison between academic years
② importance of learning foreign languages
③ strategies for improving student confidence
④ evaluation of Spanish teaching methods
⑤ offer of contract renewal for a valued teacher

19

2) 다음 글의 주제로 가장 적절한 것을 고르시오.

Peter stepped out of the freezing night air and into the brightly lit hospital lobby, holding his three-year-old daughter in his arms. The harsh light made her look even more unwell, her face all red and sweaty. Her fever had started suddenly, just before dinner, but it wouldn't go down despite his efforts. At the front desk, he explained her symptoms, his concern growing with every moment. They were quickly led to the doctor, who reassured him and carefully examined his daughter. After the doctor gave her a shot, her fever went down and she seemed more comfortable. As Peter watched her sleep peacefully that night, he felt a wave of calm wash over him.

① trust in hospital staff during emergencies
② relief after receiving medical care for a sick child
③ effects of sudden illness on family routines
④ importance of recognizing early symptoms in children
⑤ value of nighttime pediatric services

20

3) 다음 글의 주제로 가장 적절한 것을 고르시오.

Imagine you have the best tea in the world and you put it into a bag that's impermeable. It won't work. You just won't be able to make a cup of tea. For the teabag to work, it needs to be porous. You need the tea and the water to come in contact with each other. In our lives too, we cannot survive and thrive in isolation. Leaders need to be careful not to build walls around themselves that prevent people from reaching out to them. As a leader, you need to be able to touch other people. The tea was meant to mix with the water. Similarly all of us were designed to work with other people, with teams, and with society at large.

① value of openness in leadership
② necessity of clear communication channels
③ importance of having high-quality resources
④ role of consistency in organizational success
⑤ advantages of individual independence

21

4) 다음 글의 주제로 가장 적절한 것을 고르시오.

It is difficult, if not impossible, to define the limits which reason should impose on the desire for wealth; for there is no absolute or definite amount of wealth which will satisfy a man. The amount is always relative, that is to say, just so much as will maintain the proportion between what he wants and what he gets; for to measure a man's happiness only by what he gets, and not also by what he expects to get, is as pointless as to try and express a fraction which shall have a numerator but no denominator. A man never feels the loss of things which it never occurs to him to ask for; he is just as happy without them; whilst another, who may have a hundred times as much, feels miserable because he has not got the one thing he wants. In fact, every man has a horizon of his own, and he will expect as much as he thinks it is possible for him to get.

① influence of social status on personal happiness
② relativity of satisfaction in human desire for wealth
③ necessity of setting rational financial goals
④ dangers of excessive material consumption
⑤ difference between wealth and moral value

22

5) 다음 글의 주제로 가장 적절한 것을 고르시오.

All of the restaurants are using carefully chosen words to evoke vivid mental images of delicious food and rich desserts in order to draw the potential customer to their particular establishment. Just like the restaurants, nature has its own dining establishments. In a fashion similar to the restaurants' financial dependence upon drawing in many customers, the restaurateurs of the natural world (i.e., flowers) must also attract potential diners to sample their offerings. In the natural world, there are no neon signs or flashy words in which to market a potential meal to hungry animals. These restaurants that I am referring to are the world's flowers, and the potential guests are the host of organisms that visit flowers to obtain nectar and other valuable resources. Instead of using a written language or neon sign, they advertise their offerings just as effectively using the language of smell.

① comparison between restaurant marketing and customer behavior
② function of floral scents in attracting pollinators
③ development of visual advertisements in nature
④ role of written language in human advertising
⑤ importance of nutritional rewards in ecosystems

23

6) 다음 글의 주제로 가장 적절한 것을 고르시오.

Would you rather receive $1,000 in a year or $1,100 in a year and a month? Most people will opt for the larger sum in thirteen months — where else will you find a monthly interest rate of 10 percent. A wise choice, since the interest will compensate you generously for any risks you face by waiting the extra few weeks. Second question: Would you prefer $1,000 today cash on the table or $1,100 in a month? If you think like most people, you'll take the $1,000 right away. This is amazing. In both cases, if you hold out for just a month longer, you get $100 more. In the first case, it's simple enough. You figure: "I've already waited twelve months; what's one more?" Not in the second case. The introduction of "now" causes us to make inconsistent decisions. Science calls this phenomenon hyperbolic discounting. The closer a reward is, the higher our "emotional interest rate" rises and the more we are willing to give up in exchange for it.

① benefits of delayed gratification in economics
② comparison between financial and emotional investments
③ impact of immediate rewards on decision-making
④ importance of consistent financial choices
⑤ influence of risk perception on investment behavior

24

7) 다음 글의 주제로 가장 적절한 것을 고르시오.

Of central importance for understanding the development of handedness is the answer to the question of when in development it is actually determined whether a child will be left-handed or right-handed. It was long thought that handedness could only be reliably determined in elementary school, when a child learns to write. However, this assumption is incorrect. In fact, scientific studies show that left-handedness is established in many children long before elementary school — interestingly, even before birth in most people. In such studies, the hand and arm movements of unborn children in the womb are recorded using ultrasound images. Using this technique, it was shown that a clear preference for the movement of the right arm exists as early as 10 weeks after fertilization. In this study, ultrasound images of 72 unborn children 10 weeks after fertilization were evaluated and 85% showed more movements of the right arm than the left. This number is already very close to the approximately 89.4% right-handers among adults.

① influence of education on hand preference
② comparison between child and adult motor skills
③ role of writing in identifying handedness
④ prenatal emergence of handedness in humans
⑤ challenges in interpreting ultrasound data

25

8) 다음 글의 주제로 가장 적절한 것을 고르시오.

The graph above shows US dairy product imports in selected countries from 2018 to 2020. Among the four countries above, Mexico consistently recorded the highest imports of US dairy products from 2018 to 2020. However, US dairy product imports in Mexico decreased from 2019 to 2020, while the reverse was true in the other three countries during the same period. In Indonesia, US dairy product imports in 2020 were more than twice those in 2018. The increase in US dairy product imports in the Philippines from 2018 to 2019 was smaller than that in Indonesia in the same period. China was the only country where imports of US dairy products dropped between 2018 and 2019.

① comparison of dairy consumption rates worldwide
② reasons behind Mexico's declining dairy imports
③ role of trade policies in dairy product distribution
④ effects of population growth on dairy imports
⑤ trends in US dairy exports to selected countries

26

9) 다음 글의 주제로 가장 적절한 것을 고르시오.

Filippo Brunelleschi is considered to be the founding father of Renaissance architecture. He was born in Florence in 1377. Filippo was artistically talented, and trained as a goldsmith and a clockmaker before becoming an architect. When he was around 25, he traveled to Rome with his friend, the sculptor Donatello, where he studied the remains of ancient Roman buildings. His first architectural commission was the Ospedale degli Innocenti, which is one of the great Renaissance buildings. A number of other fine works, including chapels in Florentine churches, strengthened his reputation. And the stunning dome of Il Duomo is his masterpiece. He also designed machinery to produce special effects in theatrical productions. He died in Florence and was buried in Il Duomo.

① life and achievements of a pioneering Renaissance architect
② influence of Donatello on Renaissance sculpture
③ comparison between Gothic and Renaissance architecture
④ architectural symbolism of Il Duomo's dome
⑤ impact of Roman ruins on medieval engineering

27

10) 다음 글의 주제로 가장 적절한 것을 고르시오.

Youth Leaders Camp
This camp is an annual event to improve your leadership.
We look forward to meeting you soon in Canada.
Dates: July 5 – 7, 2025
Ages: 17 – 19
Place: University of Drakemont
Programs
Day 1: Team Building & Leadership Skills Workshop
Day 2: Culture Tour
Day 3: Leadership Project Planning & Presentations
Participation Fee: $700
Notes
Registration is only available online at www.ylc2025.com.
Participation fee includes everything except for the flight tickets to Canada.
For more information, please visit our website.

① promotion of a youth leadership development camp
② summary of international flight booking services
③ comparison of university leadership courses
④ announcement of a cultural exchange scholarship
⑤ review of past youth leadership programs

28

11) 다음 글의 주제로 가장 적절한 것을 고르시오.

Plogging Run
Jog, walk, pick up trash, and conserve the Earth!
When: September 13, 2025
Where: Lake Union
Details
The event starts at 11:00 a.m.
There is no participation fee.
You'll walk and run around the lake while picking up trash.
Notes
Wear comfortable athletic clothes and running shoes for your safety.
Garbage bags will be provided.
If it rains, the event will be cancelled.
If you have any questions, please email us at information@ploggingrun.org.

① tips for organizing outdoor fundraisers
② announcement of a community plogging event
③ introduction to Lake Union's ecosystem
④ guide to effective marathon training
⑤ report on local environmental pollution

29

¹²⁾ 다음 글의 주제로 가장 적절한 것을 고르시오.

In art, there are a number of ways to use perspective to obtain the illusion of depth, including using colors and graduated values of black and white, and accurately drawing the subject by applying the rules of the geometric system of perspective. In order to achieve perspective, you must make a number of observations. The forms or objects that you draw on a flat surface actually have depth and dimension in real life. As you view them and place their shapes and forms on a drawing surface, try to represent that depth to make the objects appear realistic and three-dimensional. Objects appear differently when viewed from various positions. Because of this, it's important to establish the viewpoint, and stick with it. When observing a subject, you see depth and three dimensions. When you draw this subject onto a flat surface as it appears to the eye, you are drawing in perspective.

① differences between abstract and realistic drawing styles
② role of light and shadow in artistic composition
③ techniques for creating depth through perspective in art
④ history of geometric principles in Renaissance art
⑤ challenges of drawing realistic objects without color

30

¹³⁾ 다음 글의 주제로 가장 적절한 것을 고르시오.

Low oil prices are a good thing, because it means lower energy costs of production for the majority of industries, not least the automobile and the logistics industries. Firms directly benefit from the decrease in their costs of production and provision of services. This has the effect of stimulating the aggregate supply and provides a stimulus for growth. Conversely, a sudden rise in oil prices due to a shrink in oil production is never good news, even though it definitely gives a big boost to the energy sector. A look through the history of oil price fluctuations proves this notion, as this has been the subject of much economic research. Following an oil price jump of 10 per cent due to a contraction in supply, an economy (as typified by the US economy) typically sees its output (GDP) slowed by close to 1 percentage point. For a $15 trillion economy, that is a loss of $150 billion in potential wealth or economic growth. Conversely, there has never been much concern with oil price decreases following an excess in its supply.

① history of oil production and consumption
② advantages of energy sector investment
③ risks of relying on fossil fuels for growth
④ economic impact of oil price fluctuations
⑤ differences between logistics and automobile industries

31

14) 다음 글의 주제로 가장 적절한 것을 고르시오.

We might forget an anecdote about a stranger because it makes few connections with our existing associations, but we won't forget a piece of gossip about our cousin. There's one complex network that is larger and quicker to access than all others — the self. We've been thinking about ourselves in our whole lives. (In fact, there were entire years during junior high when we weren't capable of thinking about much else.) So if a new piece of information has something to do with us, it will be more easily and thoroughly processed. It hits even closer to home than our actual home — we can take a vacation away from our home, but not from ourselves. The most effective communicators find ways to make the abstract personal. Consider the warning that law schools give to motivate first-year law students concerning the rigors of their program. Hearing that "the first-year dropout rate is 33%" is an abstract statistic. "Look to your left, look to your right. One of the three of you won't be joining us next fall" wakes up the self.

① effectiveness of personal relevance in communication
② causes of memory failure in unfamiliar situations
③ emotional impact of statistical information
④ importance of peer influence in academic success
⑤ challenges of self-awareness during adolescence

32

15) 다음 글의 주제로 가장 적절한 것을 고르시오.

Steve Jobs used analogy to get people to embrace the new technology. Before computers, people worked in a physical world. We used paper and pens and physical file folders and so on. The idea of working in a virtual world was radically different. Or at least seemed radically different. What Jobs understood was that a physical office was fundamentally similar to a virtual office. To win over the masses, Jobs drew strong analogies between the traditional workplace people knew well with the new, unfamiliar virtual workplace. In the pre-computer workplace, when ideas were written on paper it was called . . . a document. When those documents needed to be stored they were put in . . . a folder. And those folders were kept on . . . a desk. Documents, folders, and desktops are the terms we use in our virtual work because Steve Jobs understood that using familiar terms would make the new technology easier to understand. The parallels between the physical and virtual workplace now seem obvious.

① influence of design aesthetics in digital tools
② comparison between Apple and other tech companies
③ role of virtual offices in boosting productivity
④ changes in communication patterns through history
⑤ power of analogy in introducing new technology

33

16) 다음 글의 주제로 가장 적절한 것을 고르시오.

Turtle hatchlings have, it seems, evolved to crawl toward the light. For millions of years this was a highly rational and effective strategy because the light on a dark beach represented the reflection of the moon and stars on the water's surface. Following the lights led baby turtles back home to the sea. The problems started when humans began building beachfront homes and sparkling hotels on the other side of the beach. Now after hatching, turtles heading for the brightest nearby lights were being guided straight into traffic. Are self-destructive sea turtles naturally irrational? Yes, in the modern world. But there's a deeper truth. Turtles are basing their decisions on simple cues that were perfectly rational for their ancestors; these days, however, their evolved decision-making mechanisms are being blinded by modern lights.

① comparison of sea turtle behavior across species
② advantages of light sensitivity in animal navigation
③ long-term effects of coastal development on tourism
④ conflict between evolved instincts and modern environments
⑤ influence of lunar cycles on marine life

34

17) 다음 글의 주제로 가장 적절한 것을 고르시오.

Sensory organs are the only channels of communication between the brain and the outside world. Simply put, the brain is not designed to sense on its own. For instance, an exposed brain would neither sense light shining on it nor feel something touching it. In fact, patients are often kept awake during brain surgery, which can help a surgeon isolate specific regions of the brain. The ancient Greek philosopher Aristotle recognized this characteristic of the brain over 2,000 years ago when he said, "Nothing is in the mind that does not pass through the senses." This concept can be seen clearly when volunteers are blind-folded and placed in the warm water of a sensory deprivation tank. They soon experience visual, auditory, and tactile (touch) hallucinations, as well as incoherent thought patterns. From these experiments and others, it is apparent that we need constant input from our senses to carry out functions that give us personality and intellect.

① comparison of sensory functions across species
② significance of Aristotle's philosophy in neuroscience
③ dependence of mental functions on sensory input
④ advances in brain surgery techniques
⑤ dangers of sensory deprivation for physical health

35

18) 다음 글의 주제로 가장 적절한 것을 고르시오.

The writer and zoologist Desmond Morris observed that our feet communicate exactly what we think and feel more honestly than any other part of our bodies. Why are the feet and legs such accurate reflectors of our sentiments? For millions of years, long before humans spoke, our legs and feet reacted to environmental threats (e.g., hot sand, ill-tempered lions) instantaneously, without the need for conscious thought. Our limbic brains made sure that our feet and legs reacted as needed by either ceasing motion, running away, or kicking at a potential threat. This survival regimen, retained from our ancestral heritage, has served us well and continues to do so today. In fact, these age-old reactions are still so hardwired in us that when we are presented with something dangerous or even disagreeable, our feet and legs still react as they did in prehistoric times.

① development of human walking and running skills
② influence of verbal communication on human behavior
③ expression of emotion through leg and foot movement
④ role of posture in prehistoric survival
⑤ psychological interpretation of body language cues

36

19) 다음 글의 주제로 가장 적절한 것을 고르시오.

The transition from an oral culture, in which knowledge was handed down through stories, songs, and apprenticeships, to a literate one, based on the written word, was held back for centuries by the lack of suitable writing material. Stone and clay tablets were used, but they were prone to fracture and were bulky and heavy to transport. Wood suffers from splitting and is susceptible to decay. Wall paintings are static and space is limited. The invention of paper, said to be one of the four great inventions of the Chinese, solved these problems, but it wasn't until the Romans replaced the scroll with the codex — or, as we call it now, the book — that the material reached its full potential. That was two thousand years ago, and it is still a dominant form of the written word. That paper, a much softer material than either stone or wood, won out as the guardian of the written word is a remarkable materials story.

① environmental effects of early writing techniques
② decline of oral traditions in modern education
③ impact of Roman inventions on Chinese culture
④ comparison of storytelling methods in ancient societies
⑤ evolution of writing materials in human history

37

20) 다음 글의 주제로 가장 적절한 것을 고르시오.

A reason for a conclusion is very unlikely to consist in a single claim. No matter how we might state it in short-hand, it is, analytically, a complex interaction of many ideas and implications. The reason must be broken down into a chain of more precise premises. For example, the claim that 'university education should be free for all Australians' might be supported by the reason that 'the economy benefits from a well-educated Australian population'. But is our analysis of the situation clearly expressed in just one statement? Hardly. The conclusion is about universities and free education, while the reason introduces some new ideas: economic benefit and a well-educated population. While the link between these two ideas and the conclusion might seem obvious, the purpose of reasoning is to avoid assuming the 'obvious' by carefully working through the connections between the various ideas in the initial statement of our reason.

① need for analyzing complex reasoning behind conclusions
② role of education in economic development
③ benefits of making university education free
④ connection between public policy and higher education
⑤ significance of well-educated population for national progress

38

21) 다음 글의 주제로 가장 적절한 것을 고르시오.

The word "migration" is almost always reported in the popular media and even in scientific literature as a problem or a crisis. For example, migrants are assumed to overcrowd cities, clog up labor markets, and increase poverty. The other questionable assumption is that most migration is involuntary — people fleeing natural or man-made disasters. The reality, however, is more complex, and many migrants are simply seeking greater economic opportunity. Of course migration can and does create social and economic problems. But migration can also be a solution for many preexisting problems. For example, out-migration generally redistributes workers from places of labor surplus to areas where there is greater demand or more opportunity. Migration is generally selective of persons who are younger, healthier, more flexible, and more willing to endure hardship in hopes of a better life relative to their prospects in their places of origin. Most research that examines long-term outcomes of migration, including remittances and intergenerational mobility, finds positive "long-term" effects on places of origin and destination.

① causes of urban overcrowding in developing countries
② reconsideration of the commonly negative view of migration③ challenges of providing healthcare for migrant populations
④ connection between migration and international politics
⑤ historical patterns of migration across civilizations

39

22) 다음 글의 주제로 가장 적절한 것을 고르시오.

The big problem with money created by the government is that those who run the government always face the temptation to create more money and spend it. Whether among ancient kings or modern politicians, this has happened again and again over the centuries, leading to inflation and the many economic and social problems that follow from inflation. For this reason, many countries have preferred using gold, silver, or some other material that is inherently limited in supply, as money. It is a way of depriving governments of the power to expand the money supply to inflationary levels. Gold has long been considered ideal for this purpose, since the supply of gold in the world usually cannot be increased rapidly. When paper money is convertible into gold whenever the individual chooses to do so, then the money is said to be "backed up" by gold. This expression is misleading only if we imagine that the value of the gold is somehow transferred to the paper money, when in fact the real point is that the gold simply limits the amount of paper money that can be issued.

① effects of monetary policy on global trade
② risks of using limited resources as currency
③ role of gold in controlling inflation
④ comparison between modern and ancient banking systems
⑤ impact of government spending on public trust

40

23) 다음 글의 주제로 가장 적절한 것을 고르시오.

The study of emotions and decision making is now of considerable importance. This involves the application of various tools afforded by neuroscience. One important stream of the literature examines people with brain damage and how damage to particular parts of the brain known to be responsible for particular cognitive functions impacts on decision making. One example of this research is the work of Antonio Damasio, who finds that when the emotional part of the brain is damaged, this actually reduces the efficacy of decision making. Good decisions are a product of the emotional part of the brain working in conjunction with the deliberative part. This contradicts the assumptions of conventional economics, where emotions play a negative role in the decision-making process. Here it is assumed that decision making can be modeled as being generated in a stoic, unemotional fashion, and that's why decisions tend to be optimal. But the evidence suggests that emotions actually play an important and, often, a positive role in decision making.

① influence of neuroscience on economic forecasting
② limitations of traditional economic theories
③ effects of brain damage on emotional regulation
④ relationship between cognition and memory function
⑤ positive role of emotions in decision making

41~42

24) 다음 글의 주제로 가장 적절한 것을 고르시오.

Shoppers confronted with the choice of thirty different varieties of gourmet chocolates are more likely to walk away without buying any, compared with when they are presented with only half a dozen choices. If employees are given a free trip to Paris, they are happy. If you give them a free trip to Hawaii, they are happy. But if you offer them the choice between the two destinations, they are less happy, no matter what they choose. Why might choice be so disruptive? The reason is that choice forces us to make comparisons and acknowledge relative disadvantages. People who choose Paris complain that it doesn't have the ocean and those who choose Hawaii regret that it doesn't have the museums. Psychologist Barry Schwartz calls this the 'tyranny of choice' because rather than providing freedom, it actually constrains our decision-making. He argues that wider choice increases unhappiness because we worry that we are going to make the wrong decision and so we get stressed about trying to process all the comparisons in an effort to get it right. This both increases our fear of making the wrong choice and raises expectations that we should be able to get the best choice. Having made the choice, we then start to regret, wondering whether it was the right one.

① strategies for avoiding buyer's remorse
② importance of clear preferences in consumer behavior
③ comparison of decision-making styles across cultures
④ negative psychological effects of having too many choices
⑤ role of incentives in increasing employee satisfaction

43~45

25) 다음 글의 주제로 가장 적절한 것을 고르시오.

As the train pulled into a quiet countryside station, the gentle chatter of passengers filled the air. Linda was excited to finally visit her grandparents after two years. She watched people getting onto the train and hurriedly finding their seats. A moment later, an elderly woman struggled with a heavy bag, trying to sit down next to her. The bag seemed almost too big for her small body. Linda hesitated, unsure if the elderly woman would want her help. But soon, she chose to assist the woman. "Let me help you with your bag," she said. Before she could reach the bag, the elderly woman suddenly lost her balance and fell down. She lay on her back, and her face was pale. Linda froze for a moment, feeling the urgency of the situation. She quickly knelt down beside the fallen woman, as a few people rushed over. Linda carefully tapped the elderly woman's shoulder to check if she was alright. The woman groaned softly, trying to gather her strength. Linda moved closer, sliding a hand under the woman's back. As the woman's eyes slowly opened, she reassured her softly, "It's okay, just relax for a moment." Linda helped the woman sit up slowly, then guided her back to her seat. As the situation settled, people around went back to their seats. As the elderly woman finally calmed down, she looked at Linda with a smile. "I'm so sorry," she said. "I have low blood pressure, and the sudden movement of the train must have made me feel dizzy. Thank you so much for helping me." Linda nodded gently in response, then turned her gaze back to the peaceful countryside scene. She thought that no matter how unsure she might feel, even the smallest act of help is much better for someone in need than doing nothing.

① influence of childhood memories on present choices
② importance of railway safety for elderly passengers
③ effects of low blood pressure on daily life
④ challenges of traveling long distances by train
⑤ value of acting with kindness in uncertain moments

2025 고2 6월 모의고사

❶ Plus 1　❷ Plus 2　❸ Plus 3　❹ Plus 4　❺ Plus 5　❻ Plus 6　❼ Plus 7　❽ Plus 8

18

1) 다음 빈칸에 들어갈 말로 가장 적절한 것을 고르시오.

Dear Ms. Lopez,
We want to express our gratitude for your dedication as a Spanish instructor. With exceptional teaching skills, you have significantly improved our students' progress and confidence in Spanish. As the year is about to end, it is time for us to reflect on your contributions and consider the renewal of your contract. Given your positive impact, we would like to offer an extension of your contract for the next academic year. We believe ______ will further enhance our students' learning experience and academic achievement. We look forward to your response.
Sincerely,
James Martin
Principal

① your willingness to explore new teaching methods
② the school's emphasis on curriculum development
③ your continued involvement
④ your reputation as an experienced educator
⑤ the appreciation expressed by students and parents

19

2) 다음 빈칸에 들어갈 말로 가장 적절한 것을 고르시오.

Peter stepped out of the freezing night air and into the brightly lit hospital lobby, holding his three-year-old daughter in his arms. The harsh light made her look even more unwell, her face all red and sweaty. Her fever had started suddenly, just before dinner, but it wouldn't go down despite his efforts. At the front desk, he explained her symptoms, his concern growing with every moment. They were quickly led to the doctor, who reassured him and carefully examined his daughter. After the doctor gave her a shot, her fever went down and she seemed more comfortable. As Peter watched her sleep peacefully that night, he felt ______.

① an overwhelming sense of frustration from the long night
② frustrated that he hadn't taken her to the hospital earlier
③ a wave of calm wash over him
④ regretful about his earlier reactions to her illness
⑤ anxious that the fever might return at any moment

20

3) 다음 빈칸에 들어갈 말로 가장 적절한 것을 고르시오.

Imagine you have the best tea in the world and you put it into a bag that's impermeable. It won't work. You just won't be able to make a cup of tea. For the teabag to work, it needs to be porous. You need the tea and the water to come in contact with each other. In our lives too, we cannot survive and thrive in isolation. Leaders need to be careful not to build walls around themselves that prevent people from reaching out to them. As a leader, you need to be able to touch other people. The tea was meant to mix with the water. Similarly ______.

① we should protect our ideas from outside influences
② people are expected to show authority and distance
③ all of us were designed to work with other people, with teams, and with society at large
④ successful individuals must focus solely on their own goals
⑤ leaders are supposed to remain detached to maintain respect

21

4) 다음 빈칸에 들어갈 말로 가장 적절한 것을 고르시오.

It is difficult, if not impossible, to define the limits which reason should impose on the desire for wealth; for there is no absolute or definite amount of wealth which will satisfy a man. The amount is always relative, that is to say, just so much as will maintain the proportion between what he wants and what he gets; for to measure a man's happiness only by what he gets, and not also by what he expects to get, is as pointless as to try and express a fraction which shall have a numerator but no denominator. A man never feels the loss of things which it never occurs to him to ask for; he is just as happy without them; whilst another, who may have a hundred times as much, feels miserable because he has not got the one thing he wants. In fact, ______.

① people's expectations naturally decrease as they acquire more
② desire for wealth can be controlled by setting clear goals
③ every man has a horizon of his own, and he will expect as much as he thinks it is possible for him to get
④ the value of wealth lies in its ability to fulfill physical needs
⑤ there is a fixed standard of happiness based on possessions

22

5) 다음 빈칸에 들어갈 말로 가장 적절한 것을 고르시오.

All of the restaurants are using carefully chosen words to evoke vivid mental images of delicious food and rich desserts in order to draw the potential customer to their particular establishment. Just like the restaurants, nature has its own dining establishments. In a fashion similar to the restaurants' financial dependence upon drawing in many customers, the restaurateurs of the natural world (i.e., flowers) must also attract potential diners to sample their offerings. In the natural world, there are no neon signs or flashy words in which to market a potential meal to hungry animals. These restaurants that I am referring to are the world's flowers, and the potential guests are the host of organisms that visit flowers to obtain nectar and other valuable resources. Instead of using a written language or neon sign, ______.

① animals instinctively recognize flowers based on appearance alone
② flowers emit colors that resemble commercial signage
③ insects are trained to detect edible plants in the wild
④ they advertise their offerings just as effectively using the language of smell
⑤ the natural world relies on random chance for successful pollination

23

6) 다음 빈칸에 들어갈 말로 가장 적절한 것을 고르시오.

Would you rather receive $1,000 in a year or $1,100 in a year and a month? Most people will opt for the larger sum in thirteen months — where else will you find a monthly interest rate of 10 percent. A wise choice, since the interest will compensate you generously for any risks you face by waiting the extra few weeks. Second question: Would you prefer $1,000 today cash on the table or $1,100 in a month? If you think like most people, you'll take the $1,000 right away. This is amazing. In both cases, if you hold out for just a month longer, you get $100 more. In the first case, it's simple enough. You figure: "I've already waited twelve months; what's one more?" Not in the second case. ______. Science calls this phenomenon *hyperbolic discounting*. The closer a reward is, the higher our "emotional interest rate" rises and the more we are willing to give up in exchange for it.

① Our ability to calculate interest rates becomes more precise
② The smaller reward seems fairer than the delayed one
③ People value money less once it becomes available
④ The introduction of "now" causes us to make inconsistent decisions
⑤ Delayed gratification becomes easier the longer we wait

24

7) 다음 빈칸에 들어갈 말로 가장 적절한 것을 고르시오.

Of central importance for understanding the development of handedness is the answer to the question of when in development it is actually determined whether a child will be left-handed or right-handed. It was long thought that handedness could only be reliably determined in elementary school, when a child learns to write. However, this assumption is incorrect. In fact, scientific studies show that left-handedness is established in many children long before elementary school — interestingly, even before birth in most people. In such studies, the hand and arm movements of unborn children in the womb are recorded using ultrasound images. Using this technique, it was shown that a clear preference for the movement of the right arm exists as early as 10 weeks after fertilization. ______.

① This finding helps explain why children often change handedness in school
② Researchers remain unsure whether handedness is genetic or environmental
③ The consistency of this pattern supports the idea that handedness develops very early
④ Ultrasound technology has limitations in identifying arm movement in the womb
⑤ Right-handedness is more common in childhood but tends to even out in adulthood

25

8) 다음 빈칸에 들어갈 말로 가장 적절한 것을 고르시오.

The graph above shows US dairy product imports in selected countries from 2018 to 2020. Among the four countries above, Mexico consistently recorded the highest imports of US dairy products from 2018 to 2020. However, US dairy product imports in Mexico decreased from 2019 to 2020, while the reverse was true in the other three countries during the same period. In Indonesia, US dairy product imports in 2020 were more than twice those in 2018. The increase in US dairy product imports in the Philippines from 2018 to 2019 was smaller than that in Indonesia in the same period. ______.

① China saw a steady increase in US dairy product imports throughout the period
② US dairy product imports in China dropped from 2018 to 2019
③ US dairy product imports in Mexico sharply rose in 2020
④ The Philippines was the only country where imports declined during the period
⑤ Indonesia imported fewer US dairy products in 2020 than in 2019

26

9) 다음 빈칸에 들어갈 말로 가장 적절한 것을 고르시오.

Filippo Brunelleschi is considered to be ______ of Renaissance architecture. He was born in Florence in 1377. Filippo was artistically talented, and trained as a goldsmith and a clockmaker before becoming an architect. When he was around 25, he traveled to Rome with his friend, the sculptor Donatello, where he studied the remains of ancient Roman buildings. His first architectural commission was the Ospedale degli Innocenti, which is one of the great Renaissance buildings. A number of other fine works, including chapels in Florentine churches, strengthened his reputation. And the stunning dome of Il Duomo is his masterpiece. He also designed machinery to produce special effects in theatrical productions. He died in Florence and was buried in Il Duomo.

① the chief sculptor
② the founding father
③ the last artist
④ the spiritual mentor
⑤ the royal patron

27

10) 다음 빈칸에 들어갈 말로 가장 적절한 것을 고르시오.

Youth Leaders Camp
This camp is an annual event ______.
We look forward to meeting you soon in Canada.
Dates: July 5 – 7, 2025
Ages: 17 – 19
Place: University of Drakemont
Programs
Day 1: Team Building & Leadership Skills Workshop
Day 2: Culture Tour
Day 3: Leadership Project Planning & Presentations
Participation Fee: $700
Notes
Registration is only available online at www.ylc2025.com.
Participation fee includes everything except for the flight tickets to Canada.
For more information, please visit our website.

① that encourages students to explore academic fields
② for those interested in learning foreign languages
③ to improve your leadership
④ that promotes international sports competitions
⑤ to help participants find job opportunities

28

11) 다음 빈칸에 들어갈 말로 가장 적절한 것을 고르시오.

Plogging Run
Jog, walk, pick up trash, and ______!
When: September 13, 2025
Where: Lake Union
Details
The event starts at 11:00 a.m.
There is no participation fee.
You'll walk and run around the lake while picking up trash.
Notes
Wear comfortable athletic clothes and running shoes for your safety.
Garbage bags will be provided.
If it rains, the event will be cancelled.
If you have any questions, please email us at information@ploggingrun.org.

① take care of your health
② enjoy the scenic beauty
③ conserve the Earth
④ compete with fellow runners
⑤ prepare for a fitness test

29

12) 다음 빈칸에 들어갈 말로 가장 적절한 것을 고르시오.

In art, there are a number of ways to use perspective to obtain the illusion of depth, including using colors and graduated values of black and white, and accurately drawing the subject by applying the rules of the geometric system of perspective. In order to achieve perspective, you must make a number of observations. The forms or objects that you draw on a flat surface actually have depth and dimension in real life. As you view them and place their shapes and forms on a drawing surface, try to represent that depth to make the objects appear realistic and three-dimensional. ______. Because of this, it's important to establish the viewpoint, and stick with it. When observing a subject, you see depth and three dimensions. When you draw this subject onto a flat surface as it appears to the eye, you are drawing in perspective.

① Different drawing materials affect how depth is represented
② Viewers often prefer simplified images over detailed ones
③ Objects appear differently when viewed from various positions
④ It's best to use memory rather than direct observation when sketching
⑤ Perspective is less important in abstract or symbolic art

30

¹³⁾ 다음 빈칸에 들어갈 말로 가장 적절한 것을 고르시오.

Low oil prices are a good thing, because it means lower energy costs of production for the majority of industries, not least the automobile and the logistics industries. Firms directly benefit from the decrease in their costs of production and provision of services. This has the effect of stimulating the aggregate supply and provides a stimulus for growth. Conversely, a sudden rise in oil prices due to a shrink in oil production is never good news, even though it definitely gives a big boost to the energy sector. ______. Following an oil price jump of 10 per cent due to a contraction in supply, an economy (as typified by the US economy) typically sees its output (GDP) slowed by close to 1 percentage point. For a $15 trillion economy, that is a loss of $150 billion in potential wealth or economic growth. Conversely, there has never been much concern with oil price decreases following an excess in its supply.

① High oil prices are a sign of strong demand and robust economic activity
② Energy companies usually report record profits in such circumstances
③ A look through the history of oil price fluctuations proves this notion
④ Governments often intervene to stabilize oil markets when prices surge
⑤ Consumers benefit from lower oil prices through reduced utility bills

31

¹⁴⁾ 다음 빈칸에 들어갈 말로 가장 적절한 것을 고르시오.

We might forget an anecdote about a stranger because it makes few connections with our existing associations, but we won't forget a piece of gossip about our cousin. There's one complex network that is larger and quicker to access than all others — the self. We've been thinking about ourselves in our whole lives. (In fact, there were entire years during junior high when we weren't capable of thinking about much else.) So if a new piece of information has something to do with us, it will be more easily and thoroughly processed. It hits even closer to home than our actual home — we can take a vacation away from our home, but not from ourselves. ______. Consider the warning that law schools give to motivate first-year law students concerning the rigors of their program. Hearing that "the first-year dropout rate is 33%" is an abstract statistic. "Look to your left, look to your right. One of the three of you won't be joining us next fall" wakes up the self.

① Self-awareness is often a distraction in educational settings
② Making ideas relatable to people's own lives enhances communication
③ People ignore information that does not support their beliefs
④ Specific details are less persuasive than general statements
⑤ Group identity plays a stronger role than individual perspective

32

¹⁵⁾ 다음 빈칸에 들어갈 말로 가장 적절한 것을 고르시오.

Steve Jobs used analogy to get people to embrace the new technology. Before computers, people worked in a physical world. We used paper and pens and physical file folders and so on. The idea of working in a virtual world was radically different. Or at least seemed radically different. What Jobs understood was that a physical office was fundamentally similar to a virtual office. To win over the masses, Jobs drew strong analogies between the traditional workplace people knew well with the new, unfamiliar virtual workplace. In the pre-computer workplace, when ideas were written on paper it was called . . . a document. When those documents needed to be stored they were put in . . . a folder. And those folders were kept on . . . a desk. Documents, folders, and desktops are the terms we use in our virtual work because Steve Jobs understood that ______ would make the new technology easier to understand. The parallels between the physical and virtual workplace now seem obvious.

① simplifying digital tools
② imitating the structure of offices
③ using familiar terms
④ improving file management speed
⑤ avoiding technical language

33

¹⁶⁾ 다음 빈칸에 들어갈 말로 가장 적절한 것을 고르시오.

Turtle hatchlings have, it seems, evolved to crawl toward the light. For millions of years this was a highly rational and effective strategy because the light on a dark beach represented the reflection of the moon and stars on the water's surface. Following the lights led baby turtles back home to the sea. The problems started when humans began building beachfront homes and sparkling hotels on the other side of the beach. Now after hatching, turtles heading for the brightest nearby lights were being guided straight into traffic. Are self-destructive sea turtles naturally irrational? Yes, in the modern world. But there's a deeper truth. Turtles are basing their decisions on simple cues ______; these days, however, their evolved decision-making mechanisms are being blinded by modern lights.

① that continue to function well in today's environment
② that were perfectly rational for their ancestors
③ that scientists have recently discovered in hatchlings
④ that are randomly chosen by each generation of turtles
⑤ that are more complex than previously believed

34

17) 다음 빈칸에 들어갈 말로 가장 적절한 것을 고르시오.

Sensory organs are the only channels of communication between the brain and the outside world. Simply put, the brain is not designed to sense on its own. For instance, an exposed brain would neither sense light shining on it nor feel something touching it. In fact, patients are often kept awake during brain surgery, which can help a surgeon isolate specific regions of the brain. The ancient Greek philosopher Aristotle recognized this characteristic of the brain over 2,000 years ago when he said, "Nothing is in the mind that does not pass through the senses." This concept can be seen clearly when volunteers are blind-folded and placed in the warm water of a sensory deprivation tank. They soon experience visual, auditory, and tactile (touch) hallucinations, as well as incoherent thought patterns. From these experiments and others, it is apparent that ______ to carry out functions that give us personality and intellect.

① we can ignore what we see and hear
② we need constant input from our senses
③ the brain is naturally independent of stimuli
④ hallucinations occur only during sleep
⑤ people think more clearly when deprived of sensation

35

18) 다음 빈칸에 들어갈 말로 가장 적절한 것을 고르시오.

The writer and zoologist Desmond Morris observed that our feet communicate exactly what we think and feel more honestly than any other part of our bodies. Why are the feet and legs such accurate reflectors of our sentiments? For millions of years, long before humans spoke, our legs and feet reacted to environmental threats (e.g., hot sand, ill-tempered lions) instantaneously, without the need for conscious thought. Our limbic brains made sure that our feet and legs reacted as needed by either ceasing motion, running away, or kicking at a potential threat. ______. In fact, these age-old reactions are still so hardwired in us that when we are presented with something dangerous or even disagreeable, our feet and legs still react as they did in prehistoric times.

① These automatic reactions were first discovered through modern experiments
② Such physical responses are consciously controlled in high-stress situations
③ Our feet still express our feelings in the most instinctive and honest ways
④ Leg and foot gestures are culturally learned behaviors over time
⑤ Humans eventually evolved to suppress all involuntary reactions

36

19) 다음 빈칸에 들어갈 말로 가장 적절한 것을 고르시오.

The transition from an oral culture, in which knowledge was handed down through stories, songs, and apprenticeships, to a literate one, based on the written word, was held back for centuries by the lack of suitable writing material. Stone and clay tablets were used, but they were prone to fracture and were bulky and heavy to transport. Wood suffers from splitting and is susceptible to decay. Wall paintings are static and space is limited. The invention of paper, said to be one of the four great inventions of the Chinese, solved these problems, but it wasn't until the Romans replaced the scroll with the codex — or, as we call it now, the book — that the material reached its full potential. ______. That was two thousand years ago, and it is still a dominant form of the written word. That paper, a much softer material than either stone or wood, won out as the guardian of the written word is a remarkable materials story.

① Paper made it easier for artists to decorate early texts
② This transition enabled cultures to abandon oral traditions completely
③ The codex format made written information easier to access and preserve
④ Scrolls had been long preferred for their decorative and ceremonial value
⑤ Early codices were often burned or lost due to political conflict

37

20) 다음 빈칸에 들어갈 말로 가장 적절한 것을 고르시오.

A reason for a conclusion is very unlikely to consist in a single claim. No matter how we might state it in short-hand, it is, analytically, a complex interaction of many ideas and implications. The reason must be broken down into a chain of more precise premises. For example, the claim that 'university education should be free for all Australians' might be supported by the reason that 'the economy benefits from a well-educated Australian population'. But is our analysis of the situation clearly expressed in just one statement? Hardly. The conclusion is about universities and free education, while the reason introduces some new ideas: economic benefit and a well-educated population. ______. The purpose of reasoning is to avoid assuming the 'obvious' by carefully working through the connections between the various ideas in the initial statement of our reason.

① Therefore, such arguments are best left to economic experts
② In fact, this kind of claim is usually based on widely accepted facts
③ Thus, to reason properly, we must unpack the reasoning into its component parts
④ Moreover, this approach ensures that the conclusion is emotionally persuasive
⑤ So, it is safe to rely on intuitive connections when constructing arguments

38

21) 다음 빈칸에 들어갈 말로 가장 적절한 것을 고르시오.

The word "migration" is almost always reported in the popular media and even in scientific literature as a problem or a crisis. For example, migrants are assumed to overcrowd cities, clog up labor markets, and increase poverty. The other questionable assumption is that most migration is involuntary — people fleeing natural or man-made disasters. The reality, however, is more complex, and many migrants are simply seeking greater economic opportunity. Of course migration can and does create social and economic problems. ______. For example, out-migration generally redistributes workers from places of labor surplus to areas where there is greater demand or more opportunity. Migration is generally selective of persons who are younger, healthier, more flexible, and more willing to endure hardship in hopes of a better life relative to their prospects in their places of origin. Most research that examines long-term outcomes of migration, including remittances and intergenerational mobility, finds positive "long-term" effects on places of origin and destination.

① But it is rarely addressed in political discussions
② But these problems are often exaggerated by the media
③ But migration can also be a solution for many preexisting problems
④ But migrants are typically unskilled and uneducated
⑤ But governments often impose strict limits to stop it

39

22) 다음 빈칸에 들어갈 말로 가장 적절한 것을 고르시오.

The big problem with money created by the government is that those who run the government always face the temptation to create more money and spend it. Whether among ancient kings or modern politicians, this has happened again and again over the centuries, leading to inflation and the many economic and social problems that follow from inflation. For this reason, many countries have preferred using gold, silver, or some other material that is inherently limited in supply, as money. ______. Gold has long been considered ideal for this purpose, since the supply of gold in the world usually cannot be increased rapidly. When paper money is convertible into gold whenever the individual chooses to do so, then the money is said to be "backed up" by gold. This expression is misleading only if we imagine that the value of the gold is somehow transferred to the paper money, when in fact the real point is that the gold simply limits the amount of paper money that can be issued.

① This helps ensure that the public always trusts the government
② This makes it easier for banks to lend money freely
③ This prevents the public from redeeming paper money
④ This serves as a mechanism to restrain government overspending
⑤ This allows governments to manipulate the value of gold

40

23) 다음 빈칸에 들어갈 말로 가장 적절한 것을 고르시오.

The study of emotions and decision making is now of considerable importance. This involves the application of various tools afforded by neuroscience. One important stream of the literature examines people with brain damage and how damage to particular parts of the brain known to be responsible for particular cognitive functions impacts on decision making. One example of this research is the work of Antonio Damasio, who finds that when the emotional part of the brain is damaged, this actually reduces the efficacy of decision making. Good decisions are a product of the emotional part of the brain working in conjunction with the deliberative part. ______. Here it is assumed that decision making can be modeled as being generated in a stoic, unemotional fashion, and that's why decisions tend to be optimal. But the evidence suggests that emotions actually play an important and, often, a positive role in decision making.

① This view is widely accepted in modern neuroscience
② This has been confirmed by conventional economic models
③ This finding stands in sharp contrast to traditional economic theory
④ This demonstrates that emotions are harmful in uncertain situations
⑤ This reveals how optimal choices are made through logic alone

41~42

24) 다음 빈칸에 들어갈 말로 가장 적절한 것을 고르시오.

Shoppers confronted with the choice of thirty different varieties of gourmet chocolates are more likely to walk away without buying any, compared with when they are presented with only half a dozen choices. If employees are given a free trip to Paris, they are happy. If you give them a free trip to Hawaii, they are happy. But if you offer them the choice between the two destinations, they are less happy, no matter what they choose. Why might choice be so disruptive? The reason is that choice forces us to make comparisons and acknowledge relative disadvantages. People who choose Paris complain that it doesn't have the ocean and those who choose Hawaii regret that it doesn't have the museums. Psychologist Barry Schwartz calls this the 'tyranny of choice' because rather than providing freedom, it actually constrains our decision-making. He argues that wider choice increases unhappiness because we worry that we are going to make the wrong decision and so we get stressed about trying to process all the comparisons in an effort to get it right. This ______ and raises expectations that we should be able to get the best choice. Having made the choice, we then start to regret, wondering whether it was the right one.

① limits our awareness of better alternatives
② causes us to ignore the flaws of each option
③ results in emotional detachment from our decision
④ both increases our fear of making the wrong choice
⑤ prevents us from realizing the benefits of our choice

43~45

25) 다음 빈칸에 들어갈 말로 가장 적절한 것을 고르시오.

As the train pulled into a quiet countryside station, the gentle chatter of passengers filled the air. Linda was excited to finally visit her grandparents after two years. She watched people getting onto the train and hurriedly finding their seats. A moment later, an elderly woman struggled with a heavy bag, trying to sit down next to her. The bag seemed almost too big for her small body. Linda hesitated, unsure if the elderly woman would want her help. But soon, she chose to assist the woman. "Let me help you with your bag," she said. Before she could reach the bag, the elderly woman suddenly lost her balance and fell down. She lay on her back, and her face was pale. Linda froze for a moment, feeling the urgency of the situation. She quickly knelt down beside the fallen woman, as a few people rushed over. Linda carefully tapped the elderly woman's shoulder to check if she was alright. The woman groaned softly, trying to gather her strength. Linda moved closer, sliding a hand under the woman's back. As the woman's eyes slowly opened, she reassured her softly, "It's okay, just relax for a moment." Linda helped the woman sit up slowly, then guided her back to her seat. As the situation settled, people around went back to their seats. As the elderly woman finally calmed down, she looked at Linda with a smile. "I'm so sorry," she said. "I have low blood pressure, and the sudden movement of the train must have made me feel dizzy. Thank you so much for helping me." Linda nodded gently in response, then turned her gaze back to the peaceful countryside scene. She thought that ______.

① being uncertain is a sign that you should step back
② it's better to wait for others to help in emergencies
③ helping others can sometimes make things worse
④ even the smallest act of help is much better for someone in need than doing nothing
⑤ people rarely appreciate help when they're embarrassed

2025 고2 6월 모의고사

❶ Plus 1　❷ Plus 2　❸ Plus 3　❹ Plus 4　❺ Plus 5　❻ Plus 6　❼ Plus 7　❽ Plus 8

Paraphrase: 글의 파생어나 동의어를 익히며 다른 단어들로 지문을 정리하는 문제입니다. 부담 가지지 말고 채울 수 있는 곳까지 채우고 답지를 채우며 한번더 내용을 숙지해봅시다.

18

Dear Ms. Lopez,
We want to express our gratitude for your dedication as a Spanish instructor. With exceptional teaching skills, you have significantly improved our students' progress and confidence in Spanish. As the year is about to end, it is time for us to reflect on your contributions and consider the renewal of your contract. Given your positive impact, we would like to offer an extension of your contract for the next academic year. We believe
your continued involvement will further enhance our students' learning experience and academic achievement. We look forward to your response.
Sincerely,
James Martin
Principal

↓

Dear Ms. Lopez,
We would like to t__________1. you for your c__________2. as a Spanish teacher. Your excellent teaching has greatly

b__________3. our students' progress and confidence in learning Spanish. As the academic year d__________4. to a

c__________5., we are r__________6. your contributions and considering your contract renewal. Due to your positive

i__________7., we would like to e__________8. your contract for a__________9. academic year. We are confident your

continued e__________10. will further e__________11. our students' e__________12. experience and success. We look

forward to h__________13. from you.

Sincerely,

James Martin
Principal

19

Peter stepped out of the freezing night air and into the brightly lit hospital lobby, holding his three-year-old daughter in his arms. The harsh light made her look even more unwell, her face all red and sweaty. Her fever had started suddenly, just before dinner, but it wouldn't go down despite his efforts. At the front desk, he explained her symptoms, his concern growing with every moment. They were quickly led to the doctor, who reassured him and carefully examined his daughter. After the doctor gave her a shot, her fever went down and she seemed more comfortable. As Peter watched her sleep peacefully that night, he felt a wave of calm wash over him.

↓

Peter stepped out of the i__________14. night and into the brightly lit hospital lobby, c__________15. his three-year-old

daughter. The harsh lighting made her f__________16. and sweaty face look even w__________17.. Her fever had

a__________18. suddenly before dinner and r__________19. to d__________20. despite his attempts. At the r__________21.,

he explained her symptoms, his w__________22. growing. They were quickly taken to the doctor, who examined her

t__________23. and gave her an i__________24.. Her fever soon decreased, and she seemed more at e__________25..

That night, as Peter watched her sleep peacefully, he felt a deep s__________26. of r__________27..

20

Imagine you have the best tea in the world and you put it into a bag that's impermeable. It won't work. You just won't be able to make a cup of tea. For the teabag to work, it needs to be porous. You need the tea and the water to come in contact with each other. In our lives too, we cannot survive and thrive in isolation. Leaders need to be careful not to build walls around themselves that prevent people from reaching out to them. As a leader, you need to be able to touch other people. The tea was meant to mix with the water. Similarly all of us were designed to work with other people, with teams, and with society at large.

↓

Imagine having the f__________28. tea in the world but p__________29. it in a bag that doesn't let w__________30. through. The tea wouldn't b__________31.. For a teabag to f__________32., it must be porous, a__________33. the tea and water to i__________34.. In the same way, we cannot f__________35. in isolation. Leaders, in particular, should avoid creating b__________36. that keep others at a d__________37.. Effective leaders must c__________38. with those a__________39. them. Just as tea is meant to b__________40. with water, we are meant to c__________41. and e__________42. with other people, w__________43. teams and in the b__________44. community.

21

It is difficult, if not impossible, to define the limits which reason should impose on the desire for wealth; for there is no absolute or definite amount of wealth which will satisfy a man. The amount is always relative, that is to say, just so much as will maintain the proportion between what he wants and what he gets; for to measure a man's happiness only by what he gets, and not also by what he expects to get, is as pointless as to try and express a fraction which shall have a numerator but no denominator. A man never feels the loss of things which it never occurs to him to ask for; he is just as happy without them; whilst another, who may have a hundred times as much, feels miserable because he has not got the one thing he wants. In fact, every man has a horizon of his own, and he will expect as much as he thinks it is possible for him to get.

↓

It is hard—if not impossible—to s__________45. clear limits on how much reason should c__________46. a person's desire for wealth, because no f__________47. amount can truly satisfy a__________48.. S__________49. with wealth is always relative, d__________50. on the b__________51. between what a person desires and what they actually p__________52.. Measuring happiness s__________53. by what one has, w__________54. considering e__________55., is as m__________56. as trying to d__________57. a fraction without a denominator. A person doesn't m__________58. things they never thought to want and remains c__________59. without them, while someone else with v__________60. more w__________61. may feel unhappy simply because they l__________62. one specific thing they l__________63. for. Ultimately, each person has their own p__________64. horizon of desire, and their expectations a__________65. based on what they believe is a__________66..

22

All of the restaurants are using carefully chosen words to evoke vivid mental images of delicious food and rich desserts in order to draw the potential customer to their particular establishment. Just like the restaurants, nature has its own dining establishments. In a fashion similar to the restaurants' financial dependence upon drawing in many customers, the restaurateurs of the natural world (i.e., flowers) must also attract potential diners to sample their offerings. In the natural world, there are no neon signs or flashy words in which to market a potential meal to hungry animals. These restaurants that I am referring to are the world's flowers, and the potential guests are the host of organisms that visit flowers to obtain nectar and other valuable resources. Instead of using a written language or neon sign, they advertise their offerings just as effectively using the language of smell.

↓

Restaurants carefully s__________67. words to create vivid images of delicious d__________68. and t__________69. desserts to a__________70. customers. Similarly, nature has its own v__________71. of dining establishments. Just as restaurants r__________72. on drawing in many p__________73., flowers in the natural world must also l__________74. in visitors to partake in their offerings. However, in the natural world, there are no neon signs or c__________75. phrases to p__________76. a meal to hungry animals. The "restaurants" I'm referring to are flowers, and their potential guests are the v__________77. organisms that visit them for nectar and other valuable resources. Instead of written language or g__________78. signs, f__________79. advertise their offerings just as effectively through the language of s__________80..

23

Would you rather receive $1,000 in a year or $1,100 in a year and a month? Most people will opt for the larger sum in thirteen months — where else will you find a monthly interest rate of 10 percent. A wise choice, since the interest will compensate you generously for any risks you face by waiting the extra few weeks. Second question: Would you prefer $1,000 today cash on the table or $1,100 in a month? If you think like most people, you'll take the $1,000 right away. This is amazing. In both cases, if you hold out for just a month longer, you get $100 more. In the first case, it's simple enough. You figure: "I've already waited twelve months; what's one more?" Not in the second case. The introduction of "now" causes us to make inconsistent decisions. Science calls this phenomenon *hyperbolic discounting*. The closer a reward is, the higher our "emotional interest rate" rises and the more we are willing to give up in exchange for it.

↓

Would you p________81. to receive $1,000 in a year or $1,100 in a year and one month? Most people would

c________82. the larger a________83. in thirteen months — after all, where else can you e________84. a 10

percent r________85. in just one month? This is a wise d________86., as the a________87. interest more than

m________88. u________89. for the slight d________90. and any a________91. risks. Now consider this second

question: Would you r________92. have $1,000 in cash today or $1,100 a month from now? If you're like most

people, you'd likely take the $1,000 i________93.. This is fascinating because in both s________94., w________

_95. just one more month would y________96. an e________97. $100. In the first case, it feels l________98.: "I've

already waited twelve months; what's one more?" But in the second case, the i________99. of "now" leads us to

make inconsistent choices. Scientists r________100. to this behavior as hyperbolic discounting. The closer a reward is

to the p________101. moment, the higher our "emotional interest rate" becomes, and the more we're willing to

s________102. to o________103. it s________104..

24

Of central importance for understanding the development of handedness is the answer to the question of when in development it is actually determined whether a child will be
left-handed or right-handed. It was long thought that handedness could only be reliably determined in elementary school, when a child learns to write. However, this assumption is incorrect. In fact, scientific studies show that left-handedness is established in many children long before elementary school — interestingly, even before birth in most people. In such studies, the hand and arm movements of unborn children in the womb are recorded using ultrasound images. Using this technique, it was shown that a clear preference for the movement of the right arm exists as early as 10 weeks after fertilization. In this study, ultrasound images of 72 unborn children 10 weeks after fertilization were evaluated and 85% showed more movements of the right arm than the left. This number is already very close to the approximately 89.4% right-handers among adults.

↓

A k__________105. question in understanding the development of handedness is when e__________106. it is determined

whether a child will be left- or right-handed. It was once believed that handedness could only be reliably i__________

_107. during elementary school, when children b__________108. to learn writing. However, this b__________109. is

incorrect. Scientific research i__________110. that left-handedness is established in many children well before they

r__________111. school a__________112. — and, in fact, in most c__________113., even before birth. In such studies,

researchers record the movements of unborn children's hands and arms using ultrasound imaging. This method has

r__________114. that a clear preference for right-arm movements a__________115. as early as 10 weeks after fertilization.

In one such study, ultrasound s__________116. of 72 f__________117. at 10 weeks showed that 85% e__________118. more

right-arm movements than left. This p__________119. is already q__________120. close to the r__________121. 89.4% of

right-handed i__________122. in the adult p__________123..

25

The graph above shows US dairy product imports in selected countries from 2018 to 2020. Among the four countries above, Mexico consistently recorded the highest imports of US dairy products from 2018 to 2020. However, US dairy product imports in Mexico decreased from 2019 to 2020, while the reverse was true in the other three countries during the same period. In Indonesia, US dairy product imports in 2020 were more than twice those in 2018. The increase in US dairy product imports in the Philippines from 2018 to 2019 was smaller than that in Indonesia in the same period. China was the only country where imports of US dairy products dropped between 2018 and 2019.

↓

The graph above i__________124. US dairy product imports in selected countries from 2018 to 2020. O__________125. the

four countries shown, Mexico consistently had the highest v__________126. of US dairy product imports t__________127.

this p__________128.. However, imports to Mexico d__________129. from 2019 to 2020, w__________130. the other three

countries experienced i__________131. during the same t__________132.. In Indonesia, US dairy product imports in 2020

were more than d__________133. the amount recorded in 2018. The g__________134. in US dairy imports to the

Philippines from 2018 to 2019 was smaller than the i__________135. seen in Indonesia d__________136. the same period.

China was the only country where US dairy product imports d__________137. between 2018 and 2019.

26

Filippo Brunelleschi is considered to be the founding father of Renaissance architecture. He was born in Florence in 1377. Filippo was artistically talented, and trained as a goldsmith and a clockmaker before becoming an architect. When he was around 25, he traveled to Rome with his friend, the sculptor Donatello, where he studied the remains of ancient Roman buildings. His first architectural commission was the Ospedale degli Innocenti, which is one of the great Renaissance buildings. A number of other fine works, including chapels in Florentine churches, strengthened his reputation. And the stunning dome of Il Duomo is his masterpiece. He also designed machinery to produce special effects in theatrical productions. He died in Florence and was buried in Il Duomo.

↓

Filippo Brunelleschi is r__________138. as the founding father of Renaissance architecture. Born in Florence in 1377, he d__________139. artistic talent from an early age and i__________140. trained as a goldsmith and clockmaker before t__________141. to architecture. Around the age of 25, he traveled to Rome with his friend, the sculptor Donatello, where he studied the r__________142. of ancient Roman a__________143.. His first architectural p__________144. was the Ospedale degli Innocenti, now c__________145. one of the great buildings of the Renaissance. Several other n__________146. works, including chapels in churches across Florence, further e__________147. his reputation. His crowning a__________148. is the m__________149. dome of Il Duomo. Additionally, he i__________150. machinery to create special effects for theatrical p__________151.. Brunelleschi died in Florence and was l__________152. to r__________153. in Il Duomo.

27

Youth Leaders Camp
This camp is an annual event to improve your leadership.
We look forward to meeting you soon in Canada.
Dates: July 5 – 7, 2025
Ages: 17 – 19
Place: University of Drakemont
Programs
– Day 1: Team Building & Leadership Skills Workshop
– Day 2: Culture Tour
– Day 3: Leadership Project Planning & Presentations
Participation Fee: $700
Notes
– Registration is only available online at www.ylc2025.com.
– Participation fee includes everything except for the flight tickets to Canada.
For more information, please visit our website.

↓

Youth Leaders Camp

Join this annual camp designed to help you d__________154. and e__________155. your leadership skills.

We look forward to w__________156. you in Canada!

Dates: July 5–7, 2025

Ages: 17–19

Location: University of Drakemont

Program Highlights:

– Day 1: Team Building & Leadership Skills Workshop

– Day 2: Cultural Tour

– Day 3: Leadership Project Planning & Presentations

Participation Fee: $700

Important l__________157.:

Registration is available e__________158. online at www.ylc2025.com.

The participation fee c__________159. all costs except a__________160. to Canada.

For further d__________161., please visit our website.

28

Jog, walk, pick up trash, and conserve the Earth!
When: September 13, 2025
Where: Lake Union
Details
- The event starts at 11:00 a.m.
- There is no participation fee.
- You'll walk and run around the lake while picking up trash.
Notes
- Wear comfortable athletic clothes and running shoes for your safety.
- Garbage bags will be provided.
- If it rains, the event will be cancelled.
If you have any questions, please email us at information@ploggingrun.org.

↓

Jog, Walk, Pick Up Trash, and Help P___________162. the Earth!

Date: September 13, 2025

L___________163. : Lake Union

Event Details:

- The event kicks off at 11:00 a.m.

- Participation is f___________164. of c___________165..

- Participants will jog and walk around the lake while collecting l___________166..

Important Notes:

- For your safety, please wear comfortable athletic clothing and running shoes.

- Garbage bags will be provided.

- The event will be cancelled in c___________167. of rain.

If you have any questions, feel f___________168. to email us at information@ploggingrun.org.

29

In art, there are a number of ways to use perspective to obtain the illusion of depth, including using colors and graduated values of black and white, and accurately drawing the subject by applying the rules of the geometric system of perspective. In order to achieve perspective, you must make a number of observations. The forms or objects that you draw on a flat surface actually have depth and dimension in real life. As you view them and place their shapes and forms on a drawing surface, try to represent that depth to make the objects appear realistic and three-dimensional. Objects appear differently when viewed from various positions. Because of this, it's important to establish the viewpoint, and stick with it. When observing a subject, you see depth and three dimensions. When you draw this subject onto a flat surface as it appears to the eye, you are drawing in perspective.

↓

In art, there are s__________169. t__________170. to create the illusion of depth, such as using color, v__________171. shades of black and white, and accurately applying the geometric r__________172. of perspective. To effectively c__________173. perspective, careful observation is e__________174.. The objects you draw on a flat surface p__________175. actual depth and dimension in r__________176.. As you o__________177. them and t__________178. their shapes onto your drawing, a__________179. to r__________180. that depth to make the objects l__________181. realistic and three-dimensional. Objects can appear differently d__________182. on your v__________183., so it's c__________184. to choose a c__________185. viewing a__________186. and m__________187. it t__________188. your drawing. When you observe a subject, you naturally p__________189. depth and three dimensions. By c__________190. this a__________191. on a flat surface, you are p__________192. perspective drawing.

30

Low oil prices are a good thing, because it means lower energy costs of production for the majority of industries, not least the automobile and the logistics industries. Firms directly benefit from the decrease in their costs of production and provision of services. This has the effect of stimulating the aggregate supply and provides a stimulus for growth. Conversely, a sudden rise in oil prices due to a shrink in oil production is never good news, even though it definitely gives a big boost to the energy sector. A look through the history of oil price fluctuations proves this notion, as this has been the subject of much economic research. Following an oil price jump of 10 per cent due to a contraction in supply, an economy (as typified by the US economy) typically sees its output (GDP) slowed by close to 1 percentage point. For a $15 trillion economy, that is a loss of $150 billion in potential wealth or economic growth. Conversely, there has never been much concern with oil price decreases following an excess in its supply.

↓

Low oil prices are generally b__________193. as they lead to r__________194. energy costs for most industries, particularly in s__________195. like a__________196. and logistics. Companies g__________197. directly from l__________198. production and service costs, which in t__________199. stimulates aggregate supply and p__________200. economic growth. On the other hand, a sudden i__________201. in oil prices caused by reduced oil production is r__________202. positive news, even though it does s__________203. b__________204. the energy sector. Historical patterns of oil price fluctuations support this view and have been w__________205. studied in economic research. For example, when oil prices r__________206. by 10 percent due to supply c__________207., economies such as that of the US typically e__________208. a nearly 1 percentage point s__________209. in GDP growth. In a $15 trillion economy, this t__________210. to a $150 billion loss in potential wealth or economic o__________211.. In contrast, d__________212. oil prices resulting from o__________213. have r__________214. raised significant e__________215. concerns.

31

We might forget an anecdote about a stranger because it makes few connections with our existing associations, but we won't forget a piece of gossip about our cousin. There's one complex network that is larger and quicker to access than all others — the self. We've been thinking about ourselves in our whole lives. (In fact, there were entire years during junior high when we weren't capable of thinking about much else.) So if a new piece of information has something to do with *us*, it will be more easily and thoroughly processed. It hits even closer to home than our actual home — we can take a vacation away from our home, but not from *ourselves*. The most effective communicators find ways to make the abstract personal. Consider the warning that law schools give to motivate first-year law students concerning the rigors of their program. Hearing that "the first-year dropout rate is 33%" is an abstract statistic. "Look to your left, look to your right. One of the three of you won't be joining us next fall" wakes up the self.

⬇

We're likely to forget a s__________216. about a stranger because it has few connections to what we a__________217. know, but gossip about a cousin is much more m__________218.. This is because the most complex and e__________ _219. a__________220. network in our minds is the one c__________221. around ourselves. We've s__________222. our entire lives thinking about o__________223. — and at certain points, like during junior high, it often d__________224. our thoughts. When new information r__________225. to us personally, we p__________226. it more d__________227. and remember it better. In fact, it r__________228. more than anything else — we can take a vacation from our home, but n__________229. from ourselves. S__________230. communicators know this and make a__________231. ideas personal. Take, for example, how law schools motivate first-year students by h__________232. the c__________233. of the program. Simply stating, "the first-year dropout rate is 33%," is an i__________234. statistic. Saying, "Look to your left, look to your right. One of the three of you won't be here next fall," e__________235. the listener's s__________236. of s__________237. and makes the message much more impactful.

32

Steve Jobs used analogy to get people to embrace the new technology. Before computers, people worked in a physical world. We used paper and pens and physical file folders and so on. The idea of working in a virtual world was radically different. Or at least *seemed* radically different. What Jobs understood was that a physical office was fundamentally similar to a virtual office. To win over the masses, Jobs drew strong analogies between the traditional workplace people knew well with the new, unfamiliar virtual workplace. In the pre-computer workplace, when ideas were written on paper it was called . . . a document. When those documents needed to be stored they were put in . . . a folder. And those folders were kept on . . . a desk. Documents, folders, and desktops are the terms we use in our virtual work because Steve Jobs understood that using familiar terms would make the new technology easier to understand. The parallels between the physical and virtual workplace now seem obvious.

↓

Steve Jobs used analogies to help people a__________238. new technology. Before computers, work took p__________239. in a physical e__________240. — with paper, pens, file folders, and other t__________241. tools. The idea of o__________242. in a virtual world felt completely u__________243.. However, Jobs recognized that a physical office and a virtual office were fundamentally a__________244.. To make this t__________245. easier for the p__________246., he drew strong p__________247. between the w__________248. traditional workspace and the new d__________249. one. In the pre-computer office, written ideas were called documents. When these documents needed storing, they were p__________250. in folders, which were kept on a desk. These same familiar terms — documents, folders, and desktops — were a__________251. in the virtual workspace because Jobs understood that using e__________252. l__________253. would help people g__________254. the new technology more easily. Today, the s__________255. between the physical and digital o__________256. seem obvious.

33

Turtle hatchlings have, it seems, evolved to crawl toward the light. For millions of years this was a highly rational and effective strategy because the light on a dark beach represented the reflection of the moon and stars on the water's surface. Following the lights led baby turtles back home to the sea. The problems started when humans began building beachfront homes and sparkling hotels on the other side of the beach. Now after hatching, turtles heading for the brightest nearby lights were being guided straight into traffic. Are self-destructive sea turtles naturally irrational? Yes, in the modern world. But there's a deeper truth. Turtles are basing their decisions on simple cues that were perfectly rational for their ancestors; these days, however, their evolved decision-making mechanisms are being blinded by modern lights.

↓

Turtle hatchlings a__________257. to have evolved an i__________258. to move toward light. For millions of years, this behavior made perfect s__________259. — on a dark beach, light typically m__________260. the reflection of the moon and stars on the o__________261. surface. By following this light, baby turtles were g__________262. safely to the sea. Problems a__________263., however, when humans began c__________264. beachfront homes and brightly l__________ _265. hotels on the landward side of beaches. Now, n__________266. hatched turtles d__________267. to the brightest lights often h__________268. straight into d__________269. traffic. Does this make sea turtles naturally irrational? In today's world, yes. But there's a deeper point to consider: turtles r__________270. on simple cues that s__________271. their ancestors well. U__________272., in the m__________273. environment, these once-r__________274. decision-making mechanisms are being d__________275. by a__________276. lighting.

34

Sensory organs are the only channels of communication between the brain and the outside world. Simply put, the brain is not designed to sense on its own. For instance, an exposed brain would neither sense light shining on it nor feel something touching it. In fact, patients are often kept awake during brain surgery, which can help a surgeon isolate specific regions of the brain. The ancient Greek philosopher Aristotle recognized this characteristic of the brain over 2,000 years ago when he said, "Nothing is in the mind that does not pass through the senses." This concept can be seen clearly when volunteers are blind-folded and placed in the warm water of a sensory deprivation tank. They soon experience visual, auditory, and tactile (touch) hallucinations, as well as incoherent thought patterns. From these experiments and others, it is apparent that we need constant input from our senses to carry out functions that give us personality and intellect.

↓

Sensory organs serve as the brain's only m_________277. of i_________278. with the outside world. In simple terms, the brain cannot p_________279. anything by i_________280.. For example, an exposed brain would neither d_________281. light shining on it nor feel physical c_________282.. In fact, during brain surgery, patients are often kept awake to help surgeons i_________283. specific a_________284. of the brain. Over 2,000 years ago, the Greek philosopher Aristotle recognized this p_________285., stating, "Nothing is in the mind that does not pass through the senses." This idea is clearly d_________286. when volunteers are blindfolded and i_________287. in the warm water of a sensory deprivation tank. Without s_________288. input, they soon begin to experience visual, auditory, and tactile hallucinations, along with d_________289. thought patterns. Such experiments highlight the fact that c_________290. sensory input is e_________291. for m_________292. the mental p_________293. that shape our personality and intellect.

35

The writer and zoologist Desmond Morris observed that our feet communicate exactly what we think and feel more honestly than any other part of our bodies. Why are the feet and legs such accurate reflectors of our sentiments? For millions of years, long before humans spoke, our legs and feet reacted to environmental threats (e.g., hot sand, ill-tempered lions) instantaneously, without the need for conscious thought. Our limbic brains made sure that our feet and legs reacted as needed by either ceasing motion, running away, or kicking at a potential threat. This survival regimen, retained from our ancestral heritage, has served us well and continues to do so today. In fact, these age-old reactions are still so hardwired in us that when we are presented with something dangerous or even disagreeable, our feet and legs still react as they did in prehistoric times.

↓

Writer and zoologist Desmond Morris noted that our feet r__________294. our true thoughts and e__________295. more honestly than any other part of the body. But why are the feet and legs such accurate i__________296. of how we f__________297.? For millions of years, long before the a__________298. of spoken language, our legs and feet i__________299. r__________300. to environmental threats — such as scorching sand or a__________301. predators — without r__________302. conscious thought. The limbic brain e__________303. that our feet and legs reacted a__________304. by s__________305. movement, f__________306., or kicking at potential d__________307.. This survival m__________308., p__________309. down from our ancestors, has been highly e__________310. and r__________311. with us today. In fact, these a__________312. responses are so deeply i__________313. that our feet and legs still react instinctively when we e__________314. danger or d__________315., just as they did in prehistoric times.

36

The transition from an oral culture, in which knowledge was handed down through stories, songs, and apprenticeships, to a literate one, based on the written word, was held back for centuries by the lack of suitable writing material. Stone and clay tablets were used, but they were prone to fracture and were bulky and heavy to transport. Wood suffers from splitting and is susceptible to decay. Wall paintings are static and space is limited. The invention of paper, said to be one of the four great inventions of the Chinese, solved these problems, but it wasn't until the Romans replaced the scroll with the codex — or, as we call it now, the book — that the material reached its full potential. That was two thousand years ago, and it is still a dominant form of the written word. That paper, a much softer material than either stone or wood, won out as
the guardian of the written word is a remarkable materials story.

↓

The s__________316. from an oral culture—where knowledge was passed down through stories, songs, and h__________

_317. learning—to a literate c__________318. based on written t__________319. was d__________320. for centuries due to

the lack of p__________321. writing materials. E__________322. options like stone and clay tablets were f__________323.,

cumbersome, and d__________324. to transport. Wood was p__________325. to splitting and decay, while wall paintings

were i__________326. and limited by a__________327. space. The invention of paper, considered one of the four great

innovations of ancient China, a__________328. many of these i__________329.. However, it wasn't until the Romans

replaced the scroll with the codex — what we now call the book — that w__________330. material truly reached its full

potential. This i__________331. occurred two thousand years ago, and the book r__________332. a dominant form of

written c__________333.. It is a remarkable story of materials innovation that a r__________334. soft material like paper

u__________335. became the p__________336. m__________337. for p__________338. the written word.

37

A reason for a conclusion is very unlikely to consist in a single claim. No matter how we might state it in short-hand, it is, analytically, a complex interaction of many ideas and implications. The reason must be broken down into a chain of more precise premises. For example, the claim that 'university education should be free for all Australians' might be supported by the reason that 'the economy benefits from a well-educated Australian population'. But is our analysis of the situation clearly expressed in just one statement? Hardly. The conclusion is about universities and free education, while the reason introduces some new ideas: economic benefit and a well-educated population. While the link between these two ideas and the conclusion might seem obvious, the purpose of reasoning is to avoid assuming the 'obvious' by carefully working through the connections between the various ideas in the initial statement of our reason.

↓

A reason supporting a conclusion is r__________339. captured in a single s__________340.. Even if we s__________341. it b__________342., it actually involves a complex i__________343. of multiple ideas and implications. To fully u__________344. it, the reason needs to be broken down into a s__________345. of more specific premises. For instance, consider the claim that "university education should be free for all Australians." One might support this by s__________346. that "the economy benefits from a well-educated Australian population." But does this explanation really c__________347. through in just one s__________348.? Not quite. The conclusion c__________349. universities and free education, while the reason b__________350. in new c__________351. — economic benefit and an educated population. Although the c__________352. between these ideas and the conclusion may seem obvious, the g__________353. of sound reasoning is to avoid t__________354. such links for g__________355.. Instead, we must carefully e__________356. and c__________357. the r__________358. between the various e__________359. in the initial reasoning.

38

The word "migration" is almost always reported in the popular media and even in scientific literature as a problem or a crisis. For example, migrants are assumed to overcrowd cities, clog up labor markets, and increase poverty. The other questionable assumption is that most migration is involuntary — people fleeing natural or man-made disasters. The reality, however, is more complex, and many migrants are simply seeking greater economic opportunity. Of course migration can and does create social and economic problems. But migration can also be a solution for many preexisting problems. For example, out-migration generally redistributes workers from places of labor surplus to areas where there is greater demand or more opportunity. Migration is generally selective of persons who are younger, healthier, more flexible, and more willing to endure hardship in hopes of a better life relative to their prospects in their places of origin. Most research that examines long-term outcomes of migration, including remittances and intergenerational mobility, finds positive "long-term" effects on places of origin and destination.

↓

The term "migration" is often p__________360. in popular media and even in scientific literature as a problem or crisis.

Migrants are frequently assumed to overcrowd cities, s__________361. labor markets, and c__________362. to poverty.

Another common but questionable b__________363. is that most migration is involuntary — d__________364. by people

fleeing natural disasters or human-made c__________365.. In reality, the situation is more nuanced, with many migrants

simply p__________366. better economic opportunities. While migration can i__________367. lead to social and economic

c__________368., it can also help a__________369. existing problems. For example, migration often m__________370.

workers from areas with labor surpluses to r__________371. with higher demand and more opportunities. Migrants

t__________372. to be younger, healthier, more a__________373., and more willing to face d__________374. in

p__________375. of i__________376. prospects c__________377. to what they faced in their h__________378. regions. Most

research examining the long-term i__________379. of migration — including remittances and mobility a__________380.

generations — generally finds positive outcomes for both the m__________381. places of origin and their n________

_382. destinations.

39

The big problem with money created by the government is that those who run the government always face the temptation to create more money and spend it. Whether among ancient kings or modern politicians, this has happened again and again over the centuries, leading to inflation and the many economic and social problems that follow from inflation. For this reason, many countries have preferred using gold, silver, or some other material that is inherently limited in supply, as money. It is a way of depriving governments of the power to expand the money supply to inflationary levels. Gold has long been considered ideal for this purpose, since the supply of gold in the world usually cannot be increased rapidly. When paper money is convertible into gold whenever the individual chooses to do so, then the money is said to be "backed up" by gold. This expression is misleading only if we imagine that the value of the gold is somehow transferred to the paper money, when in fact the real point is that the gold simply limits the amount of paper money that can be issued.

↓

A major issue with government-i__________383. money is that those in p__________384. are often tempted to create

more of it to fund a__________385. spending. Throughout history — from ancient kings to modern politicians — this

pattern has r__________386. itself, frequently r__________387. in inflation and the many economic and social problems

that c__________388. with it. To c__________389. this risk, many countries have chosen to use gold, silver, or other

n__________390. limited materials as money. This a__________391. helps r__________392. governments from

e__________393. expanding the money supply. Gold, in particular, has long been seen as an ideal c__________394.

because its global supply typically cannot be increased q__________395.. When paper money can be e__________396. for

gold at any time by the h__________397., it is r__________398. to as being "backed by gold." This phrase can be

somewhat misleading if one a__________399. the gold d__________400. gives v__________401. to the paper money. In

reality, the key f__________402. of gold in this system is to i__________403. a limit on how much paper money can be

issued.

40

The study of emotions and decision making is now of considerable importance. This involves the application of various tools afforded by neuroscience. One important stream of the literature examines people with brain damage and how damage to particular parts of the brain known to be responsible for particular cognitive functions impacts on decision making. One example of this research is the work of Antonio Damasio, who finds that when the emotional part of the brain is damaged, this actually reduces the efficacy of decision making. Good decisions are a product of the emotional part of the brain working in conjunction with the deliberative part. This contradicts the assumptions of conventional economics, where emotions play a negative role in the decision-making process. Here it is assumed that decision making can be modeled as being generated in a stoic, unemotional fashion, and that's why decisions tend to be optimal. But the evidence suggests that emotions actually play an important and, often, a positive role in decision making.

↓

The study of emotions and decision-making has become an area of significant i__________404., with researchers now u__________405. various tools from neuroscience. A key line of research focuses on i__________406. with brain damage, examining how i__________407. to specific brain r__________408. a__________409. with particular cognitive functions a__________410. decision-making. One notable example is the work of Antonio Damasio, who discovered that damage to the emotional a__________411. of the brain actually d__________412. the q__________413. of decisions. Effective decision-making relies on the emotional and deliberative parts of the brain w__________414. together. This finding c__________415. the assumptions of t__________416. economics, which typically views emotions as d__________417. to s__________418. decision-making. According to c__________419. models, decisions are seen as optimal when they are made in a d__________420., purely r__________421. manner. However, current evidence indicates that emotions often play a v__________422. and positive role in the decision-making process.

41~42

Shoppers confronted with the choice of thirty different varieties of gourmet chocolates are more likely to walk away without buying any, compared with when they are presented with only half a dozen choices. If employees are given a free trip to Paris, they are happy. If you give them a free trip to Hawaii, they are happy. But if you offer them the choice between the two destinations, they are less happy, no matter what they choose. Why might choice be so disruptive? The reason is that choice forces us to make comparisons and acknowledge relative disadvantages. People who choose Paris complain that it doesn't have the ocean and those who choose Hawaii regret that it doesn't have the museums. Psychologist Barry Schwartz calls this the 'tyranny of choice' because rather than providing freedom, it actually constrains our decision-making. He argues that wider choice increases unhappiness because we worry that we are going to make the wrong decision and so we get stressed about trying to process all the comparisons in an effort to get it right. This both increases our fear of making the wrong choice and raises expectations that we should be able to get the best choice. Having made the choice, we
then start to regret, wondering whether it was the right one.

↓

Shoppers f_________423. with thirty different types of gourmet chocolates are less likely to make a p_________424. than when o_________425. just s_________426. options. Similarly, employees are happy when given a free trip to Paris or to Hawaii i_________427., but when asked to choose between the two, their satisfaction d_________428., r_________429. of which option they s_________430.. Why does having more choices create such d_________431.? It's because choice c_________432. us to compare options and consider their relative d_________433.. Those who pick Paris l_________434. the lack of an ocean, while those who choose Hawaii regret the a_________435. of museums. Psychologist Barry Schwartz refers to this p_________436. as the "tyranny of choice," arguing that rather than e_________437. freedom, an a_________438. of options actually h_________439. our decision-making. He suggests that more choices h_________440. unhappiness, as people become a_________441. about making the wrong choice and feel o_________442. by the comparisons involved in trying to choose the best o_________443.. After deciding, individuals often experience regret, second-guessing whether they made the right c_________444..

43~45

As the train pulled into a quiet countryside station, the gentle chatter of passengers filled the air. Linda was excited to finally visit her grandparents after two years. She watched people getting onto the train and hurriedly finding their seats. A moment later, an elderly woman struggled with a heavy bag, trying to sit down next to her. The bag seemed almost too big for her small body. Linda hesitated, unsure if the elderly woman would want her help. But soon, she chose to assist the woman. "Let me help you with your bag," she said. Before she could reach the bag, the elderly woman suddenly lost her balance and fell down. She lay on her back, and her face was pale. Linda froze for a moment, feeling the urgency of the situation. She quickly knelt down beside the fallen
woman, as a few people rushed over. Linda carefully tapped the elderly woman's shoulder to check if she was alright. The woman groaned softly, trying to gather her strength. Linda moved closer, sliding a hand under the woman's back. As the woman's eyes slowly opened, she reassured her softly, "It's okay, just relax for a moment." Linda helped the woman sit up slowly, then guided her back to her seat. As the situation settled, people around went back to their seats. As the elderly woman finally calmed down, she looked at Linda with a smile. "I'm so sorry," she said. "I have low blood pressure, and the sudden movement of the train must have made me feel dizzy. Thank you so much for helping me." Linda nodded gently in response, then turned her gaze back to the peaceful countryside scene. She thought that no matter how unsure she might feel, even the smallest act of help is much better for someone in need than doing nothing.

↓

As the train a__________445. at a quiet countryside station, the soft m__________446. of passengers filled the air. Linda was e__________447. to finally visit her grandparents after two years apart. She watched people b__________448. the train and quickly s__________449. into their seats. Moments later, an elderly woman approached, struggling with a large bag as she tried to sit b__________450. Linda. The bag appeared f__________451. too heavy for her small f__________452.. Linda hesitated, unsure if the woman would w__________453. assistance. But soon she decided to o__________454. help. "Let me help you with your bag," she said. Before she could a__________455., the elderly woman suddenly lost her balance and fell to the floor. She lay on her back, her face pale. For a moment, Linda froze, feeling the urgency of the m__________456.. Quickly r__________457. her composure, she knelt beside the woman as several others came to help. Gently, Linda tapped the woman's shoulder to check if she was c__________458.. The woman let out a soft groan as she tried to gather her strength. Moving closer, Linda slid a hand under the woman's back. As the woman's eyes slowly opened, Linda reassured her softly, "It's okay, just relax for a moment." She carefully helped the woman sit up and guided her back to her seat. Once the situation had c__________459., the other passengers r__________460. to theirs. The elderly woman, now feeling s__________461., looked at Linda with a grateful smile. "I'm so sorry," she said. "I have low blood pressure, and the train's sudden movement must have made me dizzy. Thank you so much for your help." Linda gave a gentle nod, then turned her gaze back to the peaceful countryside p__________462. by. She r__________463. that, even when unsure, o__________464. a small act of k__________465. is always better than s__________466. by and doing nothing.

2025 고2 6월 모의고사

❶ Plus 1   ❷ Plus 2   ❸ Plus 3   ❹ Plus 4   ❺ Plus 5   ❻ Plus 6   ❼ Plus 7   ❽ Plus 8

18

1. 박스 안의 보기를 재배열하여 주제문을 완성하시오.

Dear Ms. Lopez,
We want to express our gratitude for your dedication as a Spanish instructor. With exceptional teaching skills, you have significantly improved our students' progress and confidence in Spanish. As the year is about to end, it is time for us to reflect on your contributions and consider the renewal of your contract. Given your positive impact, we would like to offer an extension of your contract for the next academic year. We believe
your continued involvement will further enhance our students' learning experience and academic achievement. We look forward to your response.
Sincerely,
James Martin
Principal

A school / contract / work and / appreciates a / teacher's excellent / renew her / offers to

19

2. 박스 안의 보기를 재배열하여 주제문을 완성하시오.

Peter stepped out of the freezing night air and into the brightly lit hospital lobby, holding his three-year-old daughter in his arms. The harsh light made her look even more unwell, her face all red and sweaty. Her fever had started suddenly, just before dinner, but it wouldn't go down despite his efforts. At the front desk, he explained her symptoms, his concern growing with every moment. They were quickly led to the doctor, who reassured him and carefully examined his daughter. After the doctor gave her a shot, her fever went down and she seemed more comfortable. As Peter watched her sleep peacefully that night, he felt a wave of calm wash over him.

---

after treatment / sick daughter / A father / takes his / to the / hospital and / feels relieved

20

3. 박스 안의 보기를 재배열하여 주제문을 완성하시오.

Imagine you have the best tea in the world and you put it into a bag that's impermeable. It won't work. You just won't be able to make a cup of tea. For the teabag to work, it needs to be porous. You need the tea and the water to come in contact with each other. In our lives too, we cannot survive and thrive in isolation. Leaders need to be careful not to build walls around themselves that prevent people from reaching out to them. As a leader, you need to be able to touch other people. The tea was meant to mix with the water. Similarly all of us were designed to work with other people, with teams, and with society at large.

> need connection / water, people / isolate themselves / tea needs / must not / Just as / from others / because leaders

21

4. 박스 안의 보기를 재배열하여 주제문을 완성하시오.

It is difficult, if not impossible, to define the limits which reason should impose on the desire for wealth; for there is no absolute or definite amount of wealth which will satisfy a man. The amount is always relative, that is to say, just so much as will maintain the proportion between what he wants and what he gets; for to measure a man's happiness only by what he gets, and not also by what he expects to get, is as pointless as to try and express a fraction which shall have a numerator but no denominator. A man never feels the loss of things which it never occurs to him to ask for; he is just as happy without them; whilst another, who may have a hundred times as much, feels miserable because he has not got the one thing he wants. In fact, every man has a horizon of his own, and he will expect as much as he thinks it is possible for him to get.

> not just / possessions / Desire for / endless because / on expectations / wealth is / happiness depends

22

5. 박스 안의 보기를 재배열하여 주제문을 완성하시오.

All of the restaurants are using carefully chosen words to evoke vivid mental images of delicious food and rich desserts in order to draw the potential customer to their particular establishment. Just like the restaurants, nature has its own dining establishments. In a fashion similar to the restaurants' financial dependence upon drawing in many customers, the restaurateurs of the natural world (i.e., flowers) must also attract potential diners to sample their offerings. In the natural world, there are no neon signs or flashy words in which to market a potential meal to hungry animals. These restaurants that I am referring to are the world's flowers, and the potential guests are the host of organisms that visit flowers to obtain nectar and other valuable resources. Instead of using a written language or neon sign, they advertise their offerings just as effectively using the language of smell.

Flowers attract / use vivid / pollinators using / like restaurants / scent, much / words to / attract customers

23

6. 박스 안의 보기를 재배열하여 주제문을 완성하시오.

Would you rather receive $1,000 in a year or $1,100 in a year and a month? Most people will opt for the larger sum in thirteen months — where else will you find a monthly interest rate of 10 percent. A wise choice, since the interest will compensate you generously for any risks you face by waiting the extra few weeks. Second question: Would you prefer $1,000 today cash on the table or $1,100 in a month? If you think like most people, you'll take the $1,000 right away. This is amazing. In both cases, if you hold out for just a month longer, you get $100 more. In the first case, it's simple enough. You figure: "I've already waited twelve months; what's one more?" Not in the second case. The introduction of "now" causes us to make inconsistent decisions. Science calls this phenomenon *hyperbolic discounting*. The closer a reward is, the higher our "emotional interest rate" rises and the more we are willing to give up in exchange for it.

ones later / over larger / rewards now / People often / due to / choose smaller / emotional decision-making

24

7. 박스 안의 보기를 재배열하여 주제문을 완성하시오.

Of central importance for understanding the development of handedness is the answer to the question of when in development it is actually determined whether a child will be
left-handed or right-handed. It was long thought that handedness could only be reliably determined in elementary school, when a child learns to write. However, this assumption is incorrect. In fact, scientific studies show that left-handedness is established in many children long before elementary school — interestingly, even before birth in most people. In such studies, the hand and arm movements of unborn children in the womb are recorded using ultrasound images. Using this technique, it was shown that a clear preference for the movement of the right arm exists as early as 10 weeks after fertilization. In this study, ultrasound images of 72 unborn children 10 weeks after fertilization were evaluated and 85% showed more movements of the right arm than the left. This number is already very close to the approximately 89.4% right-handers among adults.

> studies using / Right-handedness often / fetal arm / movement / shown in / birth as / begins before

25

8. 박스 안의 보기를 재배열하여 주제문을 완성하시오.

The graph above shows US dairy product imports in selected countries from 2018 to 2020. Among the four countries above, Mexico consistently recorded the highest imports of US dairy products from 2018 to 2020. However, US dairy product imports in Mexico decreased from 2019 to 2020, while the reverse was true in the other three countries during the same period. In Indonesia, US dairy product imports in 2020 were more than twice those in 2018. The increase in US dairy product imports in the Philippines from 2018 to 2019 was smaller than that in Indonesia in the same period. China was the only country where imports of US dairy products dropped between 2018 and 2019.

> growth from / 2020 / Indonesia showed / 2018 to / imports but / U.S. dairy / Mexico led / the fastest

26

9. 박스 안의 보기를 재배열하여 주제문을 완성하시오.

Filippo Brunelleschi is considered to be the founding father of Renaissance architecture. He was born in Florence in 1377. Filippo was artistically talented, and trained as a goldsmith and a clockmaker before becoming an architect. When he was around 25, he traveled to Rome with his friend, the sculptor Donatello, where he studied the remains of ancient Roman buildings. His first architectural commission was the Ospedale degli Innocenti, which is one of the great Renaissance buildings. A number of other fine works, including chapels in Florentine churches, strengthened his reputation. And the stunning dome of Il Duomo is his masterpiece. He also designed machinery to produce special effects in theatrical productions. He died in Florence and was buried in Il Duomo.

> Renaissance architect / Brunelleschi, a / revolutionized building / design / masterpieces and / created many

27

10. 박스 안의 보기를 재배열하여 주제문을 완성하시오.

Youth Leaders Camp
This camp is an annual event to improve your leadership.
We look forward to meeting you soon in Canada.
Dates: July 5 - 7, 2025
Ages: 17 - 19
Place: University of Drakemont
Programs
- Day 1: Team Building & Leadership Skills Workshop
- Day 2: Culture Tour
- Day 3: Leadership Project Planning & Presentations
Participation Fee: $700
Notes
- Registration is only available online at www.ylc2025.com.
- Participation fee includes everything except for the flight tickets to Canada.
For more information, please visit our website.

> Camp develops / tours and / in Canada / project presentations / leadership through / Youth Leaders / teamwork, cultural

28

11. 박스 안의 보기를 재배열하여 주제문을 완성하시오.

Plogging Run
Jog, walk, pick up trash, and conserve the Earth!
When: September 13, 2025
Where: Lake Union
Details
- The event starts at 11:00 a.m.
- There is no participation fee.
- You'll walk and run around the lake while picking up trash.
Notes
- Wear comfortable athletic clothes and running shoes for your safety.
- Garbage bags will be provided.
- If it rains, the event will be cancelled.
If you have any questions, please email us at information@ploggingrun.org.

help the / pick up / Lake Union / Earth at / Join an / to jog / eco-friendly event / trash and

29

12. 박스 안의 보기를 재배열하여 주제문을 완성하시오.

In art, there are a number of ways to use perspective to obtain the illusion of depth, including using colors and graduated values of black and white, and accurately drawing the subject by applying the rules of the geometric system of perspective. In order to achieve perspective, you must make a number of observations. The forms or objects that you draw on a flat surface actually have depth and dimension in real life. As you view them and place their shapes and forms on a drawing surface, try to represent that depth to make the objects appear realistic and three-dimensional. Objects appear differently when viewed from various positions. Because of this, it's important to establish the viewpoint, and stick with it. When observing a subject, you see depth and three dimensions. When you draw this subject onto a flat surface as it appears to the eye, you are drawing in perspective.

images on / flat surfaces / perspective techniques / to draw / Artists use / realistic, three-dimensional

30

13. 박스 안의 보기를 재배열하여 주제문을 완성하시오.

Low oil prices are a good thing, because it means lower energy costs of production for the majority of industries, not least the automobile and the logistics industries. Firms directly benefit from the decrease in their costs of production and provision of services. This has the effect of stimulating the aggregate supply and provides a stimulus for growth. Conversely, a sudden rise in oil prices due to a shrink in oil production is never good news, even though it definitely gives a big boost to the energy sector. A look through the history of oil price fluctuations verifies this notion, as this has been the subject of much economic research. Following an oil price jump of 10 per cent due to a contraction in supply, an economy (as typified by the US economy) typically sees its output (GDP) slowed by close to 1 percentage point. For a $15 trillion economy, that is a loss of $150 billion in potential wealth or economic growth. Conversely, there has never been much concern with oil price decreases following an excess in its supply.

Oil price / grow while / most industries / economic output / and growth / drops help / rises reduce

---

31

14. 박스 안의 보기를 재배열하여 주제문을 완성하시오.

We might forget an anecdote about a stranger because it makes few connections with our existing associations, but we won't forget a piece of gossip about our cousin. There's one complex network that is larger and quicker to access than all others — the self. We've been thinking about ourselves in our whole lives. (In fact, there were entire years during junior high when we weren't capable of thinking about much else.) So if a new piece of information has something to do with *us*, it will be more easily and thoroughly processed. It hits even closer to home than our actual home — we can take a vacation away from our home, but not from *ourselves*. The most effective communicators find ways to make the abstract personal. Consider the warning that law schools give to motivate first-year law students concerning the rigors of their program. Hearing that "the first-year dropout rate is 33%" is an abstract statistic. "Look to your left, look to your right. One of the three of you won't be joining us next fall" wakes up the self.

---

ourselves, making / personal relevance / when it / We remember / connects to / information better / powerful

---

32

15. 박스 안의 보기를 재배열하여 주제문을 완성하시오.

Steve Jobs used analogy to get people to embrace the new technology. Before computers, people worked in a physical world. We used paper and pens and physical file folders and so on. The idea of working in a virtual world was radically different. Or at least *seemed* radically different. What Jobs understood was that a physical office was fundamentally similar to a virtual office. To win over the masses, Jobs drew strong analogies between the traditional workplace people knew well with the new, unfamiliar virtual workplace. In the pre-computer workplace, when ideas were written on paper it was called . . . a document. When those documents needed to be stored they were put in . . . a folder. And those folders were kept on . . . a desk. Documents, folders, and desktops are the terms we use in our virtual work because Steve Jobs understood that using familiar terms would make the new technology easier to understand. The parallels between the physical and virtual workplace now seem obvious.

> computer technology / used everyday / Steve Jobs / accept and / help people / analogies to / understand new

33

16. 박스 안의 보기를 재배열하여 주제문을 완성하시오.

Turtle hatchlings have, it seems, evolved to crawl toward the light. For millions of years this was a highly rational and effective strategy because the light on a dark beach represented the reflection of the moon and stars on the water's surface. Following the lights led baby turtles back home to the sea. The problems started when humans began building beachfront homes and sparkling hotels on the other side of the beach. Now after hatching, turtles heading for the brightest nearby lights were being guided straight into traffic. Are self-destructive sea turtles naturally irrational? Yes, in the modern world. But there's a deeper truth. Turtles are basing their decisions on simple cues that were perfectly rational for their ancestors; these days, however, their evolved decision-making mechanisms are being blinded by modern lights.

> the sea / misguide them / Turtles evolved / dangerously / lights now / to follow / but human / light to

34

17. 박스 안의 보기를 재배열하여 주제문을 완성하시오.

Sensory organs are the only channels of communication between the brain and the outside world. Simply put, the brain is not designed to sense on its own. For instance, an exposed brain would neither sense light shining on it nor feel something touching it. In fact, patients are often kept awake during brain surgery, which can help a surgeon isolate specific regions of the brain. The ancient Greek philosopher Aristotle recognized this characteristic of the brain over 2,000 years ago when he said, "Nothing is in the mind that does not pass through the senses." This concept can be seen clearly when volunteers are blind-folded and placed in the warm water of a sensory deprivation tank. They soon experience visual, auditory, and tactile (touch) hallucinations, as well as incoherent thought patterns. From these experiments and others, it is apparent that we need constant input from our senses to carry out functions that give us personality and intellect.

world clearly / to function / and understand / the outside / depends entirely / Our brain / on senses

35

18. 박스 안의 보기를 재배열하여 주제문을 완성하시오.

The writer and zoologist Desmond Morris observed that our feet communicate exactly what we think and feel more honestly than any other part of our bodies. Why are the feet and legs such accurate reflectors of our sentiments? For millions of years, long before humans spoke, our legs and feet reacted to environmental threats (e.g., hot sand, ill-tempered lions) instantaneously, without the need for conscious thought. Our limbic brains made sure that our feet and legs reacted as needed by either ceasing motion, running away, or kicking at a potential threat. This survival regimen, retained from our ancestral heritage, has served us well and continues to do so today. In fact, these age-old reactions are still so hardwired in us that when we are presented with something dangerous or even disagreeable, our feet and legs still react as they did in prehistoric times.

for survival / to danger / evolved to / react instantly / honest emotions / Feet reflect / because they

36

19. 박스 안의 보기를 재배열하여 주제문을 완성하시오.

The transition from an oral culture, in which knowledge was handed down through stories, songs, and apprenticeships, to a literate one, based on the written word, was held back for centuries by the lack of suitable writing material. Stone and clay tablets were used, but they were prone to fracture and were bulky and heavy to transport. Wood suffers from splitting and is susceptible to decay. Wall paintings are static and space is limited. The invention of paper, said to be one of the four great inventions of the Chinese, solved these problems, but it wasn't until the Romans replaced the scroll with the codex — or, as we call it now, the book — that the material reached its full potential. That was two thousand years ago, and it is still a dominant form of the written word. That paper, a much softer material than either stone or wood, won out as
the guardian of the written word is a remarkable materials story.

> through the / Paper replaced / books / in writing / culture spread / heavy materials / invention of / helping written

37

20. 박스 안의 보기를 재배열하여 주제문을 완성하시오.

A reason for a conclusion is very unlikely to consist in a single claim. No matter how we might state it in short-hand, it is, analytically, a complex interaction of many ideas and implications. The reason must be broken down into a chain of more precise premises. For example, the claim that 'university education should be free for all Australians' might be supported by the reason that 'the economy benefits from a well-educated Australian population'. But is our analysis of the situation clearly expressed in just one statement? Hardly. The conclusion is about universities and free education, while the reason introduces some new ideas: economic benefit and a well-educated population. While the link between these two ideas and the conclusion might seem obvious, the purpose of reasoning is to avoid assuming the 'obvious' by carefully working through the connections between the various ideas in the initial statement of our reason.

> require breaking / reasons into / down broad / Strong arguments / specific, logical / supporting ideas

38

21. 박스 안의 보기를 재배열하여 주제문을 완성하시오.

The word "migration" is almost always reported in the popular media and even in scientific literature as a problem or a crisis. For example, migrants are assumed to overcrowd cities, clog up labor markets, and increase poverty. The other questionable assumption is that most migration is involuntary — people fleeing natural or man-made disasters. The reality, however, is more complex, and many migrants are simply seeking greater economic opportunity. Of course migration can and does create social and economic problems. But migration can also be a solution for many preexisting problems. For example, out-migration generally redistributes workers from places of labor surplus to areas where there is greater demand or more opportunity. Migration is generally selective of persons who are younger, healthier, more flexible, and more willing to endure hardship in hopes of a better life relative to their prospects in their places of origin. Most research that examines long-term outcomes of migration, including remittances and intergenerational mobility, finds positive "long-term" effects on places of origin and destination.

Migration often / also offers / a crisis / redistributing labor / solutions by / and opportunity / seen as

39

22. 박스 안의 보기를 재배열하여 주제문을 완성하시오.

The big problem with money created by the government is that those who run the government always face the temptation to create more money and spend it. Whether among ancient kings or modern politicians, this has happened again and again over the centuries, leading to inflation and the many economic and social problems that follow from inflation. For this reason, many countries have preferred using gold, silver, or some other material that is inherently limited in supply, as money. It is a way of depriving governments of the power to expand the money supply to inflationary levels. Gold has long been considered ideal for this purpose, since the supply of gold in the world usually cannot be increased rapidly. When paper money is convertible into gold whenever the individual chooses to do so, then the money is said to be "backed up" by gold. This expression is misleading only if we imagine that the value of the gold is somehow transferred to the paper money, when in fact the real point is that the gold simply limits the amount of paper money that can be issued.

Limiting money / inflation caused / money / by governments / supply with / printing excess / gold prevents

40

23. 박스 안의 보기를 재배열하여 주제문을 완성하시오.

The study of emotions and decision making is now of considerable importance. This involves the application of various tools afforded by neuroscience. One important stream of the literature examines people with brain damage and how damage to particular parts of the brain known to be responsible for particular cognitive functions impacts on decision making. One example of this research is the work of Antonio Damasio, who finds that when the emotional part of the brain is damaged, this actually reduces the efficacy of decision making. Good decisions are a product of the emotional part of the brain working in conjunction with the deliberative part. This contradicts the assumptions of conventional economics, where emotions play a negative role in the decision-making process. Here it is assumed that decision making can be modeled as being generated in a stoic, unemotional fashion, and that's why decisions tend to be optimal. But the evidence suggests that emotions actually play an important and, often, a positive role in decision making.

---

best / the belief / us make / Emotions help / alone is / contrary to / better decisions / that logic

41~42

24. 박스 안의 보기를 재배열하여 주제문을 완성하시오.

Shoppers confronted with the choice of thirty different varieties of gourmet chocolates are more likely to walk away without buying any, compared with when they are presented with only half a dozen choices. If employees are given a free trip to Paris, they are happy. If you give them a free trip to Hawaii, they are happy. But if you offer them the choice between the two destinations, they are less happy, no matter what they choose. Why might choice be so disruptive? The reason is that choice forces us to make comparisons and acknowledge relative disadvantages. People who choose Paris complain that it doesn't have the ocean and those who choose Hawaii regret that it doesn't have the museums. Psychologist Barry Schwartz calls this the 'tyranny of choice' because rather than providing freedom, it actually constrains our decision-making. He argues that wider choice increases unhappiness because we worry that we are going to make the wrong decision and so we get stressed about trying to process all the comparisons in an effort to get it right. This both increases our fear of making the wrong choice and raises expectations that we should be able to get the best choice. Having made the choice, we
then start to regret, wondering whether it was the right one.

---

by increasing / decisions / fear of / choices make / regret and / Too many / making wrong / people unhappy

43~45

25. 박스 안의 보기를 재배열하여 주제문을 완성하시오.

As the train pulled into a quiet countryside station, the gentle chatter of passengers filled the air. Linda was excited to finally visit her grandparents after two years. She watched people getting onto the train and hurriedly finding their seats. A moment later, an elderly woman struggled with a heavy bag, trying to sit down next to her. The bag seemed almost too big for her small body. Linda hesitated, unsure if the elderly woman would want her help. But soon, she chose to assist the woman. "Let me help you with your bag," she said. Before she could reach the bag, the elderly woman suddenly lost her balance and fell down. She lay on her back, and her face was pale. Linda froze for a moment, feeling the urgency of the situation. She quickly knelt down beside the fallen

woman, as a few people rushed over. Linda carefully tapped the elderly woman's shoulder to check if she was alright. The woman groaned softly, trying to gather her strength. Linda moved closer, sliding a hand under the woman's back. As the woman's eyes slowly opened, she reassured her softly, "It's okay, just relax for a moment." Linda helped the woman sit up slowly, then guided her back to her seat. As the situation settled, people around went back to their seats. As the elderly woman finally calmed down, she looked at Linda with a smile. "I'm so sorry," she said. "I have low blood pressure, and the sudden movement of the train must have made me feel dizzy. Thank you so much for helping me." Linda nodded gently in response, then turned her gaze back to the peaceful countryside scene. She thought that no matter how unsure she might feel, even the smallest act of help is much better for someone in need than doing nothing.

---

learning small / in uncertain / woman on / kindnesses matter / a train / a fainting / moments / Linda helps

2025 고2 6월 모의고사

❶ Plus 1　　❷ Plus 2　　❸ Plus 3　　❹ Plus 4　　❺ Plus 5　　❻ Plus 6　　❼ Plus 7　　❽ Plus 8

18

다음 글을 요약하고자 한다. 본문의 단어를 활용하여 빈칸에 알맞은 말을 채워 넣으시오. (단, 필요 시 형태를 변화시킬 것)

Dear Ms. Lopez,
We want to express our gratitude for your dedication as a Spanish instructor. With exceptional teaching skills, you have significantly improved our students' progress and confidence in Spanish. As the year is about to end, it is time for us to reflect on your contributions and consider the renewal of your contract. Given your positive impact, we would like to offer an extension of your contract for the next academic year. We believe
your continued involvement will further enhance our students' learning experience and academic achievement. We look forward to your response.
Sincerely,
James Martin
Principal

Ms. Lopez is appreciated for i____________ 1) students' Spanish. Her c____________ 2) renewal is offered due to her positive impact and dedication.

19

다음 글을 요약하고자 한다. 본문의 단어를 활용하여 빈칸에 알맞은 말을 채워 넣으시오. (단, 필요 시 형태를 변화시킬 것)

Peter stepped out of the freezing night air and into the brightly lit hospital lobby, holding his three-year-old daughter in his arms. The harsh light made her look even more unwell, her face all red and sweaty. Her fever had started suddenly, just before dinner, but it wouldn't go down despite his efforts. At the front desk, he explained her symptoms, his concern growing with every moment. They were quickly led to the doctor, who reassured him and carefully examined his daughter. After the doctor gave her a shot, her fever went down and she seemed more comfortable. As Peter watched her sleep peacefully that night, he felt a wave of calm wash over him.

Peter rushed his feverish daughter to the hospital, where treatment eased her symptoms, bringing him c____________ 3) as she p____________ 4) slept.

20

다음 글을 요약하고자 한다. 본문의 단어를 활용하여 빈칸에 알맞은 말을 채워 넣으시오. (단, 필요 시 형태를 변화시킬 것)

Imagine you have the best tea in the world and you put it into a bag that's impermeable. It won't work. You just won't be able to make a cup of tea. For the teabag to work, it needs to be porous. You need the tea and the water to come in contact with each other. In our lives too, we cannot survive and thrive in isolation. Leaders need to be careful not to build walls around themselves that prevent people from reaching out to them. As a leader, you need to be able to touch other people. The tea was meant to mix with the water. Similarly all of us were designed to work with other people, with teams, and with society at large.

Like tea needs w__________ 5) to brew, leaders must stay open and connected, not i__________ 6), to truly grow and lead effectively.

21

다음 글을 요약하고자 한다. 본문의 단어를 활용하여 빈칸에 알맞은 말을 채워 넣으시오. (단, 필요 시 형태를 변화시킬 것)

It is difficult, if not impossible, to define the limits which reason should impose on the desire for wealth; for there is no absolute or definite amount of wealth which will satisfy a man. The amount is always relative, that is to say, just so much as will maintain the proportion between what he wants and what he gets; for to measure a man's happiness only by what he gets, and not also by what he expects to get, is as pointless as to try and express a fraction which shall have a numerator but no denominator. A man never feels the loss of things which it never occurs to him to ask for; he is just as happy without them; whilst another, who may have a hundred times as much, feels miserable because he has not got the one thing he wants. In fact, every man has a horizon of his own, and he will expect as much as he thinks it is possible for him to get.

Wealth's satisfaction is r__________ 7); happiness depends not on what one has, but on what one e__________ 8) and desires to have.

22

다음 글을 요약하고자 한다. 본문의 단어를 활용하여 빈칸에 알맞은 말을 채워 넣으시오. (단, 필요 시 형태를 변화시킬 것)

All of the restaurants are using carefully chosen words to evoke vivid mental images of delicious food and rich desserts in order to draw the potential customer to their particular establishment. Just like the restaurants, nature has its own dining establishments. In a fashion similar to the restaurants' financial dependence upon drawing in many customers, the restaurateurs of the natural world (i.e., flowers) must also attract potential diners to sample their offerings. In the natural world, there are no neon signs or flashy words in which to market a potential meal to hungry animals. These restaurants that I am referring to are the world's flowers, and the potential guests are the host of organisms that visit flowers to obtain nectar and other valuable resources. Instead of using a written language or neon sign, they advertise their offerings just as effectively using the language of smell.

> Like restaurants use words, flowers a___________9) animals with scent to offer nectar, ensuring survival through effective natural a___________10).

23

다음 글을 요약하고자 한다. 본문의 단어를 활용하여 빈칸에 알맞은 말을 채워 넣으시오. (단, 필요 시 형태를 변화시킬 것)

Would you rather receive $1,000 in a year or $1,100 in a year and a month? Most people will opt for the larger sum in thirteen months — where else will you find a monthly interest rate of 10 percent. A wise choice, since the interest will compensate you generously for any risks you face by waiting the extra few weeks. Second question: Would you prefer $1,000 today cash on the table or $1,100 in a month? If you think like most people, you'll take the $1,000 right away. This is amazing. In both cases, if you hold out for just a month longer, you get $100 more. In the first case, it's simple enough. You figure: "I've already waited twelve months; what's one more?" Not in the second case. The introduction of "now" causes us to make inconsistent decisions. Science calls this phenomenon *hyperbolic discounting*. The closer a reward is, the higher our "emotional interest rate" rises and the more we are willing to give up in exchange for it.

> People value immediate rewards more than future ones due to h___________11) discounting, leading to i___________12) financial decisions.

24

다음 글을 요약하고자 한다. 본문의 단어를 활용하여 빈칸에 알맞은 말을 채워 넣으시오. (단, 필요 시 형태를 변화시킬 것)

Of central importance for understanding the development of handedness is the answer to the question of when in development it is actually determined whether a child will be
left-handed or right-handed. It was long thought that handedness could only be reliably determined in elementary school, when a child learns to write. However, this assumption is incorrect. In fact, scientific studies show that left-handedness is established in many children long before elementary school — interestingly, even before birth in most people. In such studies, the hand and arm movements of unborn children in the womb are recorded using ultrasound images. Using this technique, it was shown that a clear preference for the movement of the right arm exists as early as 10 weeks after fertilization. In this study, ultrasound images of 72 unborn children 10 weeks after fertilization were evaluated and 85% showed more movements of the right arm than the left. This number is already very close to the approximately 89.4% right-handers among adults.

H_____________13) begins developing before birth; most unborn children show right-arm preference as early as 10 weeks after f_____________14).

25

다음 글을 요약하고자 한다. 본문의 단어를 활용하여 빈칸에 알맞은 말을 채워 넣으시오. (단, 필요 시 형태를 변화시킬 것)

The graph above shows US dairy product imports in selected countries from 2018 to 2020. Among the four countries above, Mexico consistently recorded the highest imports of US dairy products from 2018 to 2020. However, US dairy product imports in Mexico decreased from 2019 to 2020, while the reverse was true in the other three countries during the same period. In Indonesia, US dairy product imports in 2020 were more than twice those in 2018. The increase in US dairy product imports in the Philippines from 2018 to 2019 was smaller than that in Indonesia in the same period. China was the only country where imports of US dairy products dropped between 2018 and 2019.

Mexico had highest US dairy i_____________15); Indonesia saw sharp rise; China had a drop in 2019; trends varied by c_____________16) and year.

26

다음 글을 요약하고자 한다. 본문의 단어를 활용하여 빈칸에 알맞은 말을 채워 넣으시오. (단, 필요 시 형태를 변화시킬 것)

Filippo Brunelleschi is considered to be the founding father of Renaissance architecture. He was born in Florence in 1377. Filippo was artistically talented, and trained as a goldsmith and a clockmaker before becoming an architect. When he was around 25, he traveled to Rome with his friend, the sculptor Donatello, where he studied the remains of ancient Roman buildings. His first architectural commission was the Ospedale degli Innocenti, which is one of the great Renaissance buildings. A number of other fine works, including chapels in Florentine churches, strengthened his reputation. And the stunning dome of Il Duomo is his masterpiece. He also designed machinery to produce special effects in theatrical productions. He died in Florence and was buried in Il Duomo.

Filippo Brunelleschi, Renaissance a____________17) pioneer, designed Il Duomo's dome and other works after studying a____________18) Roman buildings.

27

다음 글을 요약하고자 한다. 본문의 단어를 활용하여 빈칸에 알맞은 말을 채워 넣으시오. (단, 필요 시 형태를 변화시킬 것)

Youth Leaders Camp
This camp is an annual event to improve your leadership.
We look forward to meeting you soon in Canada.
Dates: July 5 – 7, 2025
Ages: 17 – 19
Place: University of Drakemont
Programs
– Day 1: Team Building & Leadership Skills Workshop
– Day 2: Culture Tour
– Day 3: Leadership Project Planning & Presentations
Participation Fee: $700
Notes
– Registration is only available online at www.ylc2025.com.
– Participation fee includes everything except for the flight tickets to Canada.
For more information, please visit our website.

Youth Leaders Camp in Canada (July 5-7, 2025) offers l____________19) training, culture tour, and project p____________20) for ages 17-19.

28

다음 글을 요약하고자 한다. 본문의 단어를 활용하여 빈칸에 알맞은 말을 채워 넣으시오. (단, 필요 시 형태를 변화시킬 것)

Jog, walk, pick up trash, and conserve the Earth!
When: September 13, 2025
Where: Lake Union
Details
- The event starts at 11:00 a.m.
- There is no participation fee.
- You'll walk and run around the lake while picking up trash.
Notes
- Wear comfortable athletic clothes and running shoes for your safety.
- Garbage bags will be provided.
- If it rains, the event will be cancelled.
If you have any questions, please email us at information@ploggingrun.org.

Join the P____________21) Run on September 13, 2025, at Lake Union to jog, clean up trash, and help c____________22) the Earth!

29

다음 글을 요약하고자 한다. 본문의 단어를 활용하여 빈칸에 알맞은 말을 채워 넣으시오. (단, 필요 시 형태를 변화시킬 것)

In art, there are a number of ways to use perspective to obtain the illusion of depth, including using colors and graduated values of black and white, and accurately drawing the subject by applying the rules of the geometric system of perspective. In order to achieve perspective, you must make a number of observations. The forms or objects that you draw on a flat surface actually have depth and dimension in real life. As you view them and place their shapes and forms on a drawing surface, try to represent that depth to make the objects appear realistic and three-dimensional. Objects appear differently when viewed from various positions. Because of this, it's important to establish the viewpoint, and stick with it. When observing a subject, you see depth and three dimensions. When you draw this subject onto a flat surface as it appears to the eye, you are drawing in perspective.

To create depth in art, observe real-life dimensions, set a v____________23), and apply perspective rules for realistic, three-d____________24) drawings.

30

다음 글을 요약하고자 한다. 본문의 단어를 활용하여 빈칸에 알맞은 말을 채워 넣으시오. (단, 필요 시 형태를 변화시킬 것)

Low oil prices are a good thing, because it means lower energy costs of production for the majority of industries, not least the automobile and the logistics industries. Firms directly benefit from the decrease in their costs of production and provision of services. This has the effect of stimulating the aggregate supply and provides a stimulus for growth. Conversely, a sudden rise in oil prices due to a shrink in oil production is never good news, even though it definitely gives a big boost to the energy sector. A look through the history of oil price fluctuations verifies this notion, as this has been the subject of much economic research. Following an oil price jump of 10 per cent due to a contraction in supply, an economy (as typified by the US economy) typically sees its output (GDP) slowed by close to 1 percentage point. For a $15 trillion economy, that is a loss of $150 billion in potential wealth or economic growth. Conversely, there has never been much concern with oil price decreases following an excess in its supply.

> Low oil prices lower production c____________25) and boost growth, while price hikes reduce GDP despite benefiting the e____________26) sector.

31

다음 글을 요약하고자 한다. 본문의 단어를 활용하여 빈칸에 알맞은 말을 채워 넣으시오. (단, 필요 시 형태를 변화시킬 것)

We might forget an anecdote about a stranger because it makes few connections with our existing associations, but we won't forget a piece of gossip about our cousin. There's one complex network that is larger and quicker to access than all others — the self. We've been thinking about ourselves in our whole lives. (In fact, there were entire years during junior high when we weren't capable of thinking about much else.) So if a new piece of information has something to do with *us*, it will be more easily and thoroughly processed. It hits even closer to home than our actual home — we can take a vacation away from our home, but not from *ourselves*. The most effective communicators find ways to make the abstract personal. Consider the warning that law schools give to motivate first-year law students concerning the rigors of their program. Hearing that "the first-year dropout rate is 33%" is an abstract statistic. "Look to your left, look to your right. One of the three of you won't be joining us next fall" wakes up the self.

> We remember information better when it relates to ourselves; personal c____________27) make a____________28) ideas more memorable and impactful.

32

다음 글을 요약하고자 한다. 본문의 단어를 활용하여 빈칸에 알맞은 말을 채워 넣으시오. (단, 필요 시 형태를 변화시킬 것)

Steve Jobs used analogy to get people to embrace the new technology. Before computers, people worked in a physical world. We used paper and pens and physical file folders and so on. The idea of working in a virtual world was radically different. Or at least *seemed* radically different. What Jobs understood was that a physical office was fundamentally similar to a virtual office. To win over the masses, Jobs drew strong analogies between the traditional workplace people knew well with the new, unfamiliar virtual workplace. In the pre-computer workplace, when ideas were written on paper it was called . . . a document. When those documents needed to be stored they were put in . . . a folder. And those folders were kept on . . . a desk. Documents, folders, and desktops are the terms we use in our virtual work because Steve Jobs understood that using familiar terms would make the new technology easier to understand. The parallels between the physical and virtual workplace now seem obvious.

Steve Jobs used familiar a___________29) like documents and folders to help people understand and accept the new v___________30) computer world.

33

다음 글을 요약하고자 한다. 본문의 단어를 활용하여 빈칸에 알맞은 말을 채워 넣으시오. (단, 필요 시 형태를 변화시킬 것)

Turtle hatchlings have, it seems, evolved to crawl toward the light. For millions of years this was a highly rational and effective strategy because the light on a dark beach represented the reflection of the moon and stars on the water's surface. Following the lights led baby turtles back home to the sea. The problems started when humans began building beachfront homes and sparkling hotels on the other side of the beach. Now after hatching, turtles heading for the brightest nearby lights were being guided straight into traffic. Are self-destructive sea turtles naturally irrational? Yes, in the modern world. But there's a deeper truth. Turtles are basing their decisions on simple cues that were perfectly rational for their ancestors; these days, however, their evolved decision-making mechanisms are being blinded by modern lights.

Turtle h___________31) follow light to reach the sea, but modern artificial lights mislead them, showing e___________32) cues can become harmful today.

34

다음 글을 요약하고자 한다. 본문의 단어를 활용하여 빈칸에 알맞은 말을 채워 넣으시오. (단, 필요 시 형태를 변화시킬 것)

Sensory organs are the only channels of communication between the brain and the outside world. Simply put, the brain is not designed to sense on its own. For instance, an exposed brain would neither sense light shining on it nor feel something touching it. In fact, patients are often kept awake during brain surgery, which can help a surgeon isolate specific regions of the brain. The ancient Greek philosopher Aristotle recognized this characteristic of the brain over 2,000 years ago when he said, "Nothing is in the mind that does not pass through the senses." This concept can be seen clearly when volunteers are blind-folded and placed in the warm water of a sensory deprivation tank. They soon experience visual, auditory, and tactile (touch) hallucinations, as well as incoherent thought patterns. From these experiments and others, it is apparent that we need constant input from our senses to carry out functions that give us personality and intellect.

> The brain relies on s____________33) organs for input; without them, it can't sense or think clearly, highlighting senses' role in m____________34) and self.

35

다음 글을 요약하고자 한다. 본문의 단어를 활용하여 빈칸에 알맞은 말을 채워 넣으시오. (단, 필요 시 형태를 변화시킬 것)

The writer and zoologist Desmond Morris observed that our feet communicate exactly what we think and feel more honestly than any other part of our bodies. Why are the feet and legs such accurate reflectors of our sentiments? For millions of years, long before humans spoke, our legs and feet reacted to environmental threats (e.g., hot sand, ill-tempered lions) instantaneously, without the need for conscious thought. Our limbic brains made sure that our feet and legs reacted as needed by either ceasing motion, running away, or kicking at a potential threat. This survival regimen, retained from our ancestral heritage, has served us well and continues to do so today. In fact, these age-old reactions are still so hardwired in us that when we are presented with something dangerous or even disagreeable, our feet and legs still react as they did in prehistoric times.

> Our feet and legs reveal true feelings, reacting instinctively to t____________35) due to ancient survival instincts h____________36) in the brain.

36

다음 글을 요약하고자 한다. 본문의 단어를 활용하여 빈칸에 알맞은 말을 채워 넣으시오. (단, 필요 시 형태를 변화시킬 것)

The transition from an oral culture, in which knowledge was handed down through stories, songs, and apprenticeships, to a literate one, based on the written word, was held back for centuries by the lack of suitable writing material. Stone and clay tablets were used, but they were prone to fracture and were bulky and heavy to transport. Wood suffers from splitting and is susceptible to decay. Wall paintings are static and space is limited. The invention of paper, said to be one of the four great inventions of the Chinese, solved these problems, but it wasn't until the Romans replaced the scroll with the codex — or, as we call it now, the book — that the material reached its full potential. That was two thousand years ago, and it is still a dominant form of the written word. That paper, a much softer material than either stone or wood, won out as
the guardian of the written word is a remarkable materials story.

> Paper enabled the shift from oral to l____________37) culture by solving limitations of earlier materials; books remain key to w___________38) communication.

37

다음 글을 요약하고자 한다. 본문의 단어를 활용하여 빈칸에 알맞은 말을 채워 넣으시오. (단, 필요 시 형태를 변화시킬 것)

A reason for a conclusion is very unlikely to consist in a single claim. No matter how we might state it in short-hand, it is, analytically, a complex interaction of many ideas and implications. The reason must be broken down into a chain of more precise premises. For example, the claim that 'university education should be free for all Australians' might be supported by the reason that 'the economy benefits from a well-educated Australian population'. But is our analysis of the situation clearly expressed in just one statement? Hardly. The conclusion is about universities and free education, while the reason introduces some new ideas: economic benefit and a well-educated population. While the link between these two ideas and the conclusion might seem obvious, the purpose of reasoning is to avoid assuming the 'obvious' by carefully working through the connections between the various ideas in the initial statement of our reason.

> Sound reasoning requires breaking down c___________39) reasons into clear, connected premises, rather than relying on oversimplified or a___________40) links.

38

다음 글을 요약하고자 한다. 본문의 단어를 활용하여 빈칸에 알맞은 말을 채워 넣으시오. (단, 필요 시 형태를 변화시킬 것)

The word "migration" is almost always reported in the popular media and even in scientific literature as a problem or a crisis. For example, migrants are assumed to overcrowd cities, clog up labor markets, and increase poverty. The other questionable assumption is that most migration is involuntary — people fleeing natural or man-made disasters. The reality, however, is more complex, and many migrants are simply seeking greater economic opportunity. Of course migration can and does create social and economic problems. But migration can also be a solution for many preexisting problems. For example, out-migration generally redistributes workers from places of labor surplus to areas where there is greater demand or more opportunity. Migration is generally selective of persons who are younger, healthier, more flexible, and more willing to endure hardship in hopes of a better life relative to their prospects in their places of origin. Most research that examines long-term outcomes of migration, including remittances and intergenerational mobility, finds positive "long-term" effects on places of origin and destination.

> Migration is often seen as a problem, but it also solves l___________41) imbalances and offers long-term benefits to both origin and d___________42) regions.

39

다음 글을 요약하고자 한다. 본문의 단어를 활용하여 빈칸에 알맞은 말을 채워 넣으시오. (단, 필요 시 형태를 변화시킬 것)

The big problem with money created by the government is that those who run the government always face the temptation to create more money and spend it. Whether among ancient kings or modern politicians, this has happened again and again over the centuries, leading to inflation and the many economic and social problems that follow from inflation. For this reason, many countries have preferred using gold, silver, or some other material that is inherently limited in supply, as money. It is a way of depriving governments of the power to expand the money supply to inflationary levels. Gold has long been considered ideal for this purpose, since the supply of gold in the world usually cannot be increased rapidly. When paper money is convertible into gold whenever the individual chooses to do so, then the money is said to be "backed up" by gold. This expression is misleading only if we imagine that the value of the gold is somehow transferred to the paper money, when in fact the real point is that the gold simply limits the amount of paper money that can be issued.

> Gold limits i___________43) by restricting paper money supply, preventing g___________44) from overspending and causing economic instability over time.

40

다음 글을 요약하고자 한다. 본문의 단어를 활용하여 빈칸에 알맞은 말을 채워 넣으시오. (단, 필요 시 형태를 변화시킬 것)

The study of emotions and decision making is now of considerable importance. This involves the application of various tools afforded by neuroscience. One important stream of the literature examines people with brain damage and how damage to particular parts of the brain known to be responsible for particular cognitive functions impacts on decision making. One example of this research is the work of Antonio Damasio, who finds that when the emotional part of the brain is damaged, this actually reduces the efficacy of decision making. Good decisions are a product of the emotional part of the brain working in conjunction with the deliberative part. This contradicts the assumptions of conventional economics, where emotions play a negative role in the decision-making process. Here it is assumed that decision making can be modeled as being generated in a stoic, unemotional fashion, and that's why decisions tend to be optimal. But the evidence suggests that emotions actually play an important and, often, a positive role in decision making.

Emotions, once seen as n____________45) in decision making, are now shown to enhance it when working with rational thought, especially in n____________46) studies.

41~42

다음 글을 요약하고자 한다. 본문의 단어를 활용하여 빈칸에 알맞은 말을 채워 넣으시오. (단, 필요 시 형태를 변화시킬 것)

Shoppers confronted with the choice of thirty different varieties of gourmet chocolates are more likely to walk away without buying any, compared with when they are presented with only half a dozen choices. If employees are given a free trip to Paris, they are happy. If you give them a free trip to Hawaii, they are happy. But if you offer them the choice between the two destinations, they are less happy, no matter what they choose. Why might choice be so disruptive? The reason is that choice forces us to make comparisons and acknowledge relative disadvantages. People who choose Paris complain that it doesn't have the ocean and those who choose Hawaii regret that it doesn't have the museums. Psychologist Barry Schwartz calls this the 'tyranny of choice' because rather than providing freedom, it actually constrains our decision-making. He argues that wider choice increases unhappiness because we worry that we are going to make the wrong decision and so we get stressed about trying to process all the comparisons in an effort to get it right. This both increases our fear of making the wrong choice and raises expectations that we should be able to get the best choice. Having made the choice, we then start to regret, wondering whether it was the right one.

Too many choices can cause stress, r____________47), and dissatisfaction; this "t____________48) of choice" makes decisions harder and less satisfying.

43~45

다음 글을 요약하고자 한다. 본문의 단어를 활용하여 빈칸에 알맞은 말을 채워 넣으시오. (단, 필요 시 형태를 변화시킬 것)

As the train pulled into a quiet countryside station, the gentle chatter of passengers filled the air. Linda was excited to finally visit her grandparents after two years. She watched people getting onto the train and hurriedly finding their seats. A moment later, an elderly woman struggled with a heavy bag, trying to sit down next to her. The bag seemed almost too big for her small body. Linda hesitated, unsure if the elderly woman would want her help. But soon, she chose to assist the woman. "Let me help you with your bag," she said. Before she could reach the bag, the elderly woman suddenly lost her balance and fell down. She lay on her back, and her face was pale. Linda froze for a moment, feeling the urgency of the situation. She quickly knelt down beside the fallen
woman, as a few people rushed over. Linda carefully tapped the elderly woman's shoulder to check if she was alright. The woman groaned softly, trying to gather her strength. Linda moved closer, sliding a hand under the woman's back. As the woman's eyes slowly opened, she reassured her softly, "It's okay, just relax for a moment." Linda helped the woman sit up slowly, then guided her back to her seat. As the situation settled, people around went back to their seats. As the elderly woman finally calmed down, she looked at Linda with a smile. "I'm so sorry," she said. "I have low blood pressure, and the sudden movement of the train must have made me feel dizzy. Thank you so much for helping me." Linda nodded gently in response, then turned her gaze back to the peaceful countryside scene. She thought that no matter how unsure she might feel, even the smallest act of help is much better for someone in need than doing nothing.

Linda helped a fainting e____________49) woman on the train, realizing that even small acts of kindness matter more than h____________50) or doubt.

2025 고2 6월 모의고사

❶ Plus 1　**❷ Plus 2**　**❸ Plus 3**　**❹ Plus 4**　**❺ Plus 5**　**❻ Plus 6**　**❼ Plus 7**　**❽ Plus 8**

18

다음 글의 내용을 요약하고자 한다. 빈칸에 들어갈 말로 적절한 것은?

Dear Ms. Lopez,
We want to express our gratitude for your dedication as a Spanish instructor. With exceptional teaching skills, you have significantly improved our students' progress and confidence in Spanish. As the year is about to end, it is time for us to reflect on your contributions and consider the renewal of your contract. Given your positive impact, we would like to offer an extension of your contract for the next academic year. We believe
your continued involvement will further enhance our students' learning experience and academic achievement. We look forward to your response.
Sincerely,
James Martin
Principal

↓

*조건> 선택형이 아닌 주관식형 문제는 본문에 있는 단어를 활용하여 쓸 것

Ms. Lopez is appreciated for her teaching. Her impact ______________51) students' Spanish. The school offers a contract ______________52), expecting c______________53) contribution to student learning and achievement.

19

다음 글의 내용을 요약하고자 한다. 빈칸에 들어갈 말로 적절한 것은?

Peter stepped out of the freezing night air and into the brightly lit hospital lobby, holding his three-year-old daughter in his arms. The harsh light made her look even more unwell, her face all red and sweaty. Her fever had started suddenly, just before dinner, but it wouldn't go down despite his efforts. At the front desk, he explained her symptoms, his concern growing with every moment. They were quickly led to the doctor, who reassured him and carefully examined his daughter. After the doctor gave her a shot, her fever went down and she seemed more comfortable. As Peter watched her sleep peacefully that night, he felt a wave of calm wash over him.

↓

*조건> 선택형이 아닌 주관식형 문제는 본문에 있는 단어를 활용하여 쓸 것

Peter took his sick daughter to the hospital. After the doctor's shot, her ______________54) went down. Watching her sleep p______________55), he finally felt c______________56) and relieved.

20

다음 글의 내용을 요약하고자 한다. 빈칸에 들어갈 말로 적절한 것은?

Imagine you have the best tea in the world and you put it into a bag that's impermeable. It won't work. You just won't be able to make a cup of tea. For the teabag to work, it needs to be porous. You need the tea and the water to come in contact with each other. In our lives too, we cannot survive and thrive in isolation. Leaders need to be careful not to build walls around themselves that prevent people from reaching out to them. As a leader, you need to be able to touch other people. The tea was meant to mix with the water. Similarly all of us were designed to work with other people, with teams, and with society at large.

↓

*조건> 선택형이 아닌 주관식형 문제는 본문에 있는 단어를 활용하여 쓸 것

Like tea needs ____________ 57) with water, people, especially ____________ 58), must connect with others. We're meant to live, work, and grow together—not in ____________ 59) from society or teams.

21

다음 글의 내용을 요약하고자 한다. 빈칸에 들어갈 말로 적절한 것은?

It is difficult, if not impossible, to define the limits which reason should impose on the desire for wealth; for there is no absolute or definite amount of wealth which will satisfy a man. The amount is always relative, that is to say, just so much as will maintain the proportion between what he wants and what he gets; for to measure a man's happiness only by what he gets, and not also by what he expects to get, is as pointless as to try and express a fraction which shall have a numerator but no denominator. A man never feels the loss of things which it never occurs to him to ask for; he is just as happy without them; whilst another, who may have a hundred times as much, feels miserable because he has not got the one thing he wants. In fact, every man has a horizon of his own, and he will expect as much as he thinks it is possible for him to get.

↓

*조건> 선택형이 아닌 주관식형 문제는 본문에 있는 단어를 활용하여 쓸 것

Desire for wealth has [X / no]60) fixed limit. Happiness depends not just on what one gets, but on e____________ 61). Each person feels content or miserable based on their own mental ____________ 62).

22

다음 글의 내용을 요약하고자 한다. 빈칸에 들어갈 말로 적절한 것은?

All of the restaurants are using carefully chosen words to evoke vivid mental images of delicious food and rich desserts in order to draw the potential customer to their particular establishment. Just like the restaurants, nature has its own dining establishments. In a fashion similar to the restaurants' financial dependence upon drawing in many customers, the restaurateurs of the natural world (i.e., flowers) must also attract potential diners to sample their offerings. In the natural world, there are no neon signs or flashy words in which to market a potential meal to hungry animals. These restaurants that I am referring to are the world's flowers, and the potential guests are the host of organisms that visit flowers to obtain nectar and other valuable resources. Instead of using a written language or neon sign, they advertise their offerings just as effectively using the language of smell.

↓

*조건> 선택형이 아닌 주관식형 문제는 본문에 있는 단어를 활용하여 쓸 것

Like restaurants ______________63) customers with ______________64), flowers attract animals with smell. Without signs or language, flowers ______________65) nectar to potential diners in the natural world through scent.

23

다음 글의 내용을 요약하고자 한다. 빈칸에 들어갈 말로 적절한 것은?

Would you rather receive $1,000 in a year or $1,100 in a year and a month? Most people will opt for the larger sum in thirteen months — where else will you find a monthly interest rate of 10 percent. A wise choice, since the interest will compensate you generously for any risks you face by waiting the extra few weeks. Second question: Would you prefer $1,000 today cash on the table or $1,100 in a month? If you think like most people, you'll take the $1,000 right away. This is amazing. In both cases, if you hold out for just a month longer, you get $100 more. In the first case, it's simple enough. You figure: "I've already waited twelve months; what's one more?" Not in the second case. The introduction of "now" causes us to make inconsistent decisions. Science calls this phenomenon *hyperbolic discounting*. The closer a reward is, the higher our "emotional interest rate" rises and the more we are willing to give up in exchange for it.

↓

*조건> 선택형이 아닌 주관식형 문제는 본문에 있는 단어를 활용하여 쓸 것

People often choose [**immediate** / **gradual**]66) rewards over better future ones due to h______________67) d______________68), where ______________69) interest increases as rewards get closer, causing ______________70) and short-sighted decisions.

24

다음 글의 내용을 요약하고자 한다. 빈칸에 들어갈 말로 적절한 것은?

Of central importance for understanding the development of handedness is the answer to the question of when in development it is actually determined whether a child will be
left-handed or right-handed. It was long thought that handedness could only be reliably determined in elementary school, when a child learns to write. However, this assumption is incorrect. In fact, scientific studies show that left-handedness is established in many children long before elementary school — interestingly, even before birth in most people. In such studies, the hand and arm movements of unborn children in the womb are recorded using ultrasound images. Using this technique, it was shown that a clear preference for the movement of the right arm exists as early as 10 weeks after fertilization. In this study, ultrasound images of 72 unborn children 10 weeks after fertilization were evaluated and 85% showed more movements of the right arm than the left. This number is already very close to the approximately 89.4% right-handers among adults.

↓

*조건> 선택형이 아닌 주관식형 문제는 본문에 있는 단어를 활용하여 쓸 것

Handedness develops [**before** / **after**]71) birth. Studies using _____________72) show most unborn children prefer _____________73) arm movement by 10 weeks, matching adult right-handedness rates. Writing age isn't the true indicator.

25

다음 글의 내용을 요약하고자 한다. 빈칸에 들어갈 말로 적절한 것은?

The graph above shows US dairy product imports in selected countries from 2018 to 2020. Among the four countries above, Mexico consistently recorded the highest imports of US dairy products from 2018 to 2020. However, US dairy product imports in Mexico decreased from 2019 to 2020, while the reverse was true in the other three countries during the same period. In Indonesia, US dairy product imports in 2020 were more than twice those in 2018. The increase in US dairy product imports in the Philippines from 2018 to 2019 was smaller than that in Indonesia in the same period. China was the only country where imports of US dairy products dropped between 2018 and 2019.

↓

*조건> 선택형이 아닌 주관식형 문제는 본문에 있는 단어를 활용하여 쓸 것

From 2018 to 2020, Mexico led in US _____________74) imports. Indonesia saw big [**increases** / **decreases**]75), China had a [**rise** / **drop**]76) in 2019, and the Philippines' growth was [**bigger** / **smaller**]77) than Indonesia's.

26

다음 글의 내용을 요약하고자 한다. 빈칸에 들어갈 말로 적절한 것은?

Filippo Brunelleschi is considered to be the founding father of Renaissance architecture. He was born in Florence in 1377. Filippo was artistically talented, and trained as a goldsmith and a clockmaker before becoming an architect. When he was around 25, he traveled to Rome with his friend, the sculptor Donatello, where he studied the remains of ancient Roman buildings. His first architectural commission was the Ospedale degli Innocenti, which is one of the great Renaissance buildings. A number of other fine works, including chapels in Florentine churches, strengthened his reputation. And the stunning dome of Il Duomo is his masterpiece. He also designed machinery to produce special effects in theatrical productions. He died in Florence and was buried in Il Duomo.

*조건> 선택형이 아닌 주관식형 문제는 본문에 있는 단어를 활용하여 쓸 것

Filippo Brunelleschi, born in Florence, studied ____________78) buildings and became a key Renaissance ____________79). His masterpiece is Il Duomo's dome. He also created stage ____________80) and was buried there.

27

다음 글의 내용을 요약하고자 한다. 빈칸에 들어갈 말로 적절한 것은?

Youth Leaders Camp
This camp is an annual event to improve your leadership.
We look forward to meeting you soon in Canada.
Dates: July 5 - 7, 2025
Ages: 17 - 19
Place: University of Drakemont
Programs
- Day 1: Team Building & Leadership Skills Workshop
- Day 2: Culture Tour
- Day 3: Leadership Project Planning & Presentations
Participation Fee: $700
Notes
- Registration is only available online at www.ylc2025.com.
- Participation fee includes everything except for the flight tickets to Canada.
For more information, please visit our website.

*조건> 선택형이 아닌 주관식형 문제는 본문에 있는 단어를 활용하여 쓸 것

Youth Leaders Camp in Canada (July 5-7, 2025) offers teens ____________81) workshops, a ____________82) tour, and ____________83) planning. $700 covers all but flight. Online registration required at website.

28

다음 글의 내용을 요약하고자 한다. 빈칸에 들어갈 말로 적절한 것은?

Jog, walk, pick up trash, and conserve the Earth!
When: September 13, 2025
Where: Lake Union
Details
- The event starts at 11:00 a.m.
- There is no participation fee.
- You'll walk and run around the lake while picking up trash.
Notes
- Wear comfortable athletic clothes and running shoes for your safety.
- Garbage bags will be provided.
- If it rains, the event will be cancelled.
If you have any questions, please email us at information@ploggingrun.org.

↓

*조건> 선택형이 아닌 주관식형 문제는 본문에 있는 단어를 활용하여 쓸 것

Join the ______________84) Run at Lake Union on September 13, 2025. Walk, jog, and pick up trash. F____________85) event starts at 11 a.m. Bags p____________86). Canceled if it rains.

29

다음 글의 내용을 요약하고자 한다. 빈칸에 들어갈 말로 적절한 것은?

In art, there are a number of ways to use perspective to obtain the illusion of depth, including using colors and graduated values of black and white, and accurately drawing the subject by applying the rules of the geometric system of perspective. In order to achieve perspective, you must make a number of observations. The forms or objects that you draw on a flat surface actually have depth and dimension in real life. As you view them and place their shapes and forms on a drawing surface, try to represent that depth to make the objects appear realistic and three-dimensional. Objects appear differently when viewed from various positions. Because of this, it's important to establish the viewpoint, and stick with it. When observing a subject, you see depth and three dimensions. When you draw this subject onto a flat surface as it appears to the eye, you are drawing in perspective.

↓

*조건> 선택형이 아닌 주관식형 문제는 본문에 있는 단어를 활용하여 쓸 것

To create ______________87) in art, use ______________88) with color, value, and geometry. Observe real-life forms, fix a ______________89), and draw them realistically on a flat surface with ______________90)-dimensional effect.

30

다음 글의 내용을 요약하고자 한다. 빈칸에 들어갈 말로 적절한 것은?

Low oil prices are a good thing, because it means lower energy costs of production for the majority of industries, not least the automobile and the logistics industries. Firms directly benefit from the decrease in their costs of production and provision of services. This has the effect of stimulating the aggregate supply and provides a stimulus for growth. Conversely, a sudden rise in oil prices due to a shrink in oil production is never good news, even though it definitely gives a big boost to the energy sector. A look through the history of oil price fluctuations verifies this notion, as this has been the subject of much economic research. Following an oil price jump of 10 per cent due to a contraction in supply, an economy (as typified by the US economy) typically sees its output (GDP) slowed by close to 1 percentage point. For a $15 trillion economy, that is a loss of $150 billion in potential wealth or economic growth. Conversely, there has never been much concern with oil price decreases following an excess in its supply.

↓

*조건> 선택형이 아닌 주관식형 문제는 본문에 있는 단어를 활용하여 쓸 것

Low oil prices [**raise** / **lower**]91) production c______________92) and [**boost** / **hinder**]93) growth. In contrast, sudden price rises from [**increased** / **reduced**]94) supply slow GDP. History shows supply cuts harm economies, while e____________95) supply brings little concern.

31

다음 글의 내용을 요약하고자 한다. 빈칸에 들어갈 말로 적절한 것은?

We might forget an anecdote about a stranger because it makes few connections with our existing associations, but we won't forget a piece of gossip about our cousin. There's one complex network that is larger and quicker to access than all others — the self. We've been thinking about ourselves in our whole lives. (In fact, there were entire years during junior high when we weren't capable of thinking about much else.) So if a new piece of information has something to do with *us*, it will be more easily and thoroughly processed. It hits even closer to home than our actual home — we can take a vacation away from our home, but not from *ourselves*. The most effective communicators find ways to make the abstract personal. Consider the warning that law schools give to motivate first-year law students concerning the rigors of their program. Hearing that "the first-year dropout rate is 33%" is an abstract statistic. "Look to your left, look to your right. One of the three of you won't be joining us next fall" wakes up the self.

↓

*조건> 선택형이 아닌 주관식형 문제는 본문에 있는 단어를 활용하여 쓸 것

We remember self-related information better. Personal [**connections** / **separations**]96) help processing. Effective communicators make ______________97) ideas ______________98), like turning statistics into [**relatable** / **relative**]99) examples to engage the self more deeply.

32

다음 글의 내용을 요약하고자 한다. 빈칸에 들어갈 말로 적절한 것은?

Steve Jobs used analogy to get people to embrace the new technology. Before computers, people worked in a physical world. We used paper and pens and physical file folders and so on. The idea of working in a virtual world was radically different. Or at least *seemed* radically different. What Jobs understood was that a physical office was fundamentally similar to a virtual office. To win over the masses, Jobs drew strong analogies between the traditional workplace people knew well with the new, unfamiliar virtual workplace. In the pre-computer workplace, when ideas were written on paper it was called . . . a document. When those documents needed to be stored they were put in . . . a folder. And those folders were kept on . . . a desk. Documents, folders, and desktops are the terms we use in our virtual work because Steve Jobs understood that using familiar terms would make the new technology easier to understand. The parallels between the physical and virtual workplace now seem obvious.

↓

*조건> 선택형이 아닌 주관식형 문제는 본문에 있는 단어를 활용하여 쓸 것

Steve Jobs used ____________100) to connect physical and ____________101) workplaces. By using [familiar / new]102) terms like document, folder, and desktop, he made new technology easier for people to ____________103) and accept.

33

다음 글의 내용을 요약하고자 한다. 빈칸에 들어갈 말로 적절한 것은?

Turtle hatchlings have, it seems, evolved to crawl toward the light. For millions of years this was a highly rational and effective strategy because the light on a dark beach represented the reflection of the moon and stars on the water's surface. Following the lights led baby turtles back home to the sea. The problems started when humans began building beachfront homes and sparkling hotels on the other side of the beach. Now after hatching, turtles heading for the brightest nearby lights were being guided straight into traffic. Are self-destructive sea turtles naturally irrational? Yes, in the modern world. But there's a deeper truth. Turtles are basing their decisions on simple cues that were perfectly rational for their ancestors; these days, however, their evolved decision-making mechanisms are being blinded by modern lights.

↓

*조건> 선택형이 아닌 주관식형 문제는 본문에 있는 단어를 활용하여 쓸 것

Turtle ____________104) evolved to follow natural light to the sea. But modern artificial lights mislead them. Though once ____________105), their inherited ____________106) cues now cause danger in today's world.

34

다음 글의 내용을 요약하고자 한다. 빈칸에 들어갈 말로 적절한 것은?

Sensory organs are the only channels of communication between the brain and the outside world. Simply put, the brain is not designed to sense on its own. For instance, an exposed brain would neither sense light shining on it nor feel something touching it. In fact, patients are often kept awake during brain surgery, which can help a surgeon isolate specific regions of the brain. The ancient Greek philosopher Aristotle recognized this characteristic of the brain over 2,000 years ago when he said, "Nothing is in the mind that does not pass through the senses." This concept can be seen clearly when volunteers are blind-folded and placed in the warm water of a sensory deprivation tank. They soon experience visual, auditory, and tactile (touch) hallucinations, as well as incoherent thought patterns. From these experiments and others, it is apparent that we need constant input from our senses to carry out functions that give us personality and intellect.

↓

*조건> 선택형이 아닌 주관식형 문제는 본문에 있는 단어를 활용하여 쓸 것

The brain [can / cannot]107) sense without ___________108) organs. Experiments like sensory deprivation tanks show that without c___________109) sensory input, thought and perception become distorted, proving senses shape mind and intellect.

35

다음 글의 내용을 요약하고자 한다. 빈칸에 들어갈 말로 적절한 것은?

The writer and zoologist Desmond Morris observed that our feet communicate exactly what we think and feel more honestly than any other part of our bodies. Why are the feet and legs such accurate reflectors of our sentiments? For millions of years, long before humans spoke, our legs and feet reacted to environmental threats (e.g., hot sand, ill-tempered lions) instantaneously, without the need for conscious thought. Our limbic brains made sure that our feet and legs reacted as needed by either ceasing motion, running away, or kicking at a potential threat. This survival regimen, retained from our ancestral heritage, has served us well and continues to do so today. In fact, these age-old reactions are still so hardwired in us that when we are presented with something dangerous or even disagreeable, our feet and legs still react as they did in prehistoric times.

↓

*조건> 선택형이 아닌 주관식형 문제는 본문에 있는 단어를 활용하여 쓸 것

Our feet and legs h___________110) ___________111) feelings. Evolved for survival, they react instantly to threats [with / without]112) thought. These ancient limbic responses remain ___________113) and still influence our behavior today.

36

다음 글의 내용을 요약하고자 한다. 빈칸에 들어갈 말로 적절한 것은?

The transition from an oral culture, in which knowledge was handed down through stories, songs, and apprenticeships, to a literate one, based on the written word, was held back for centuries by the lack of suitable writing material. Stone and clay tablets were used, but they were prone to fracture and were bulky and heavy to transport. Wood suffers from splitting and is susceptible to decay. Wall paintings are static and space is limited. The invention of paper, said to be one of the four great inventions of the Chinese, solved these problems, but it wasn't until the Romans replaced the scroll with the codex — or, as we call it now, the book — that the material reached its full potential. That was two thousand years ago, and it is still a dominant form of the written word. That paper, a much softer material than either stone or wood, won out as the guardian of the written word is a remarkable materials story.

↓

*조건> 선택형이 아닌 주관식형 문제는 본문에 있는 단어를 활용하여 쓸 것

The shift from ____________ 114) to ____________ 115) culture was delayed by [suitable / poor]116) writing materials. Paper and the codex solved this, making the book a lasting and d____________ 117) form of written knowledge.

37

다음 글의 내용을 요약하고자 한다. 빈칸에 들어갈 말로 적절한 것은?

A reason for a conclusion is very unlikely to consist in a single claim. No matter how we might state it in short-hand, it is, analytically, a complex interaction of many ideas and implications. The reason must be broken down into a chain of more precise premises. For example, the claim that 'university education should be free for all Australians' might be supported by the reason that 'the economy benefits from a well-educated Australian population'. But is our analysis of the situation clearly expressed in just one statement? Hardly. The conclusion is about universities and free education, while the reason introduces some new ideas: economic benefit and a well-educated population. While the link between these two ideas and the conclusion might seem obvious, the purpose of reasoning is to avoid assuming the 'obvious' by carefully working through the connections between the various ideas in the initial statement of our reason.

↓

*조건> 선택형이 아닌 주관식형 문제는 본문에 있는 단어를 활용하여 쓸 것

A reason for a conclusion is ____________ 118), not a single claim. Good reasoning breaks it into ____________ 119) premises, [involving / avoiding]120) assumptions and clearly connecting ideas like education, economy, and public benefit.

38

다음 글의 내용을 요약하고자 한다. 빈칸에 들어갈 말로 적절한 것은?

The word "migration" is almost always reported in the popular media and even in scientific literature as a problem or a crisis. For example, migrants are assumed to overcrowd cities, clog up labor markets, and increase poverty. The other questionable assumption is that most migration is involuntary — people fleeing natural or man-made disasters. The reality, however, is more complex, and many migrants are simply seeking greater economic opportunity. Of course migration can and does create social and economic problems. But migration can also be a solution for many preexisting problems. For example, out-migration generally redistributes workers from places of labor surplus to areas where there is greater demand or more opportunity. Migration is generally selective of persons who are younger, healthier, more flexible, and more willing to endure hardship in hopes of a better life relative to their prospects in their places of origin. Most research that examines long-term outcomes of migration, including remittances and intergenerational mobility, finds positive "long-term" effects on places of origin and destination.

↓

*조건> 선택형이 아닌 주관식형 문제는 본문에 있는 단어를 활용하여 쓸 것

_______________121) is often seen as a crisis, but many seek _______________122). Though problems exist, migration can solve _______________123) imbalances and bring long-term benefits to both origin and _______________124) areas.

39

다음 글의 내용을 요약하고자 한다. 빈칸에 들어갈 말로 적절한 것은?

The big problem with money created by the government is that those who run the government always face the temptation to create more money and spend it. Whether among ancient kings or modern politicians, this has happened again and again over the centuries, leading to inflation and the many economic and social problems that follow from inflation. For this reason, many countries have preferred using gold, silver, or some other material that is inherently limited in supply, as money. It is a way of depriving governments of the power to expand the money supply to inflationary levels. Gold has long been considered ideal for this purpose, since the supply of gold in the world usually cannot be increased rapidly. When paper money is convertible into gold whenever the individual chooses to do so, then the money is said to be "backed up" by gold. This expression is misleading only if we imagine that the value of the gold is somehow transferred to the paper money, when in fact the real point is that the gold simply limits the amount of paper money that can be issued.

↓

*조건> 선택형이 아닌 주관식형 문제는 본문에 있는 단어를 활용하여 쓸 것

Government-created money risks _______________125) due to overspending. Gold's [unlimited / limited]126) supply prevents this. Gold-backed money restricts issuance, not by transferring value, but by l_______________127) excessive paper money creation.

40

다음 글의 내용을 요약하고자 한다. 빈칸에 들어갈 말로 적절한 것은?

The study of emotions and decision making is now of considerable importance. This involves the application of various tools afforded by neuroscience. One important stream of the literature examines people with brain damage and how damage to particular parts of the brain known to be responsible for particular cognitive functions impacts on decision making. One example of this research is the work of Antonio Damasio, who finds that when the emotional part of the brain is damaged, this actually reduces the efficacy of decision making. Good decisions are a product of the emotional part of the brain working in conjunction with the deliberative part. This contradicts the assumptions of conventional economics, where emotions play a negative role in the decision-making process. Here it is assumed that decision making can be modeled as being generated in a stoic, unemotional fashion, and that's why decisions tend to be optimal. But the evidence suggests that emotions actually play an important and, often, a positive role in decision making.

↓

*조건> 선택형이 아닌 주관식형 문제는 본문에 있는 단어를 활용하여 쓸 것

Neuroscience shows ______________128) improve ______________129) making. Brain damage studies, like Damasio's, reveal emotional and ______________130) parts must work together, [supporting / challenging]131) economics' view that emotions harm rational decisions.

41~42

다음 글의 내용을 요약하고자 한다. 빈칸에 들어갈 말로 적절한 것은?

Shoppers confronted with the choice of thirty different varieties of gourmet chocolates are more likely to walk away without buying any, compared with when they are presented with only half a dozen choices. If employees are given a free trip to Paris, they are happy. If you give them a free trip to Hawaii, they are happy. But if you offer them the choice between the two destinations, they are less happy, no matter what they choose. Why might choice be so disruptive? The reason is that choice forces us to make comparisons and acknowledge relative disadvantages. People who choose Paris complain that it doesn't have the ocean and those who choose Hawaii regret that it doesn't have the museums. Psychologist Barry Schwartz calls this the 'tyranny of choice' because rather than providing freedom, it actually constrains our decision-making. He argues that wider choice increases unhappiness because we worry that we are going to make the wrong decision and so we get stressed about trying to process all the comparisons in an effort to get it right. This both increases our fear of making the wrong choice and raises expectations that we should be able to get the best choice. Having made the choice, we
then start to regret, wondering whether it was the right one.

↓

*조건> 선택형이 아닌 주관식형 문제는 본문에 있는 단어를 활용하여 쓸 것

Too many choices can [increase / reduce]132) happiness. The " ______________133) of choice" causes stress, regret, and fear of wrong decisions, as people compare options and focus on what each [has / lacks]134) after choosing.

43~45

다음 글의 내용을 요약하고자 한다. 빈칸에 들어갈 말로 적절한 것은?

As the train pulled into a quiet countryside station, the gentle chatter of passengers filled the air. Linda was excited to finally visit her grandparents after two years. She watched people getting onto the train and hurriedly finding their seats. A moment later, an elderly woman struggled with a heavy bag, trying to sit down next to her. The bag seemed almost too big for her small body. Linda hesitated, unsure if the elderly woman would want her help. But soon, she chose to assist the woman. "Let me help you with your bag," she said. Before she could reach the bag, the elderly woman suddenly lost her balance and fell down. She lay on her back, and her face was pale. Linda froze for a moment, feeling the urgency of the situation. She quickly knelt down beside the fallen woman, as a few people rushed over. Linda carefully tapped the elderly woman's shoulder to check if she was alright. The woman groaned softly, trying to gather her strength. Linda moved closer, sliding a hand under the woman's back. As the woman's eyes slowly opened, she reassured her softly, "It's okay, just relax for a moment." Linda helped the woman sit up slowly, then guided her back to her seat. As the situation settled, people around went back to their seats. As the elderly woman finally calmed down, she looked at Linda with a smile. "I'm so sorry," she said. "I have low blood pressure, and the sudden movement of the train must have made me feel dizzy. Thank you so much for helping me." Linda nodded gently in response, then turned her gaze back to the peaceful countryside scene. She thought that no matter how unsure she might feel, even the smallest act of help is much better for someone in need than doing nothing.

↓

*조건> 선택형이 아닌 주관식형 문제는 본문에 있는 단어를 활용하여 쓸 것

On a train, Linda helped an ______________135) woman who fainted from dizziness. Despite her h______________136), she acted with care, realizing that small acts of help truly matter in u______________137) situations.

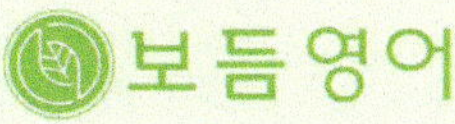

정답

WORK BOOK

2025 시행 고2 6월 모의고사 내신대비용 WorkBook & 변형문제

1) [정답] ②
해설
reflect on your contributions는 문맥상 Ms. Lopez가 그동안 수업에서 학생들의 성취에 기여한 바를 되돌아보고 평가한다는 의미로 사용되었다. 이는 단순히 수치를 평가하거나 비교하는 것이 아니라, 그녀의 전반적인 영향과 가치를 깊이 있게 생각해본다는 뜻이다. 따라서 think carefully about the value of your work(자신의 일의 가치를 깊이 생각하다)가 가장 적절한 해석이다.
①은 출석 기록 측정으로 contributions(기여도)와는 관계가 없다. ③은 시험 결과만 평가하는 좁은 해석으로 contributions의 폭넓은 의미와 맞지 않는다. ④는 타 교사와 비교하는 내용으로 지문에 그런 의도가 나타나지 않는다. ⑤는 계약 조건 논의로 지문 후반에 언급되지만 reflect on your contributions라는 표현의 직접적 의미와는 다르다.

2) [정답] ③
해설
a wave of calm wash over him은 문맥상 딸의 열이 내리고 평온하게 잠든 모습을 본 후 피터가 느낀 강한 안도감을 묘사하는 표현이다. 긴장과 걱정이 가득했던 상황에서 걱정이 풀리며 마음이 평온해지는 감정의 변화를 나타낸다. 따라서 experienced a strong feeling of relief(강한 안도감을 느꼈다)가 가장 적절한 해석이다.
①은 피로감으로 해석되지만 본문은 감정적 변화에 중점을 두고 있다. ②는 치료에 대한 의심을 나타내지만, 피터는 오히려 평온함을 느꼈다. ④는 딸을 지켜보고 싶은 마음이지만 calm wash over him과는 직접 연결되지 않는다. ⑤는 자신의 유년 시절 기억을 떠올렸다는 내용은 지문에 언급되지 않는다.

3) [정답] ⑤
해설
build walls around themselves는 문맥상 리더들이 스스로를 고립시키고 다른 사람들과의 소통과 교류를 차단하는 것을 의미한다. 지문에서는 이런 태도가 리더십에 부정적이라는 점을 강조하며, 리더는 다른 사람들과 접촉하고 협력해야 한다고 말하고 있다. 따라서 isolate themselves and limit communication with others(자신을 고립시키고 타인과의 소통을 제한한다)가 가장 적절한 해석이다.
①은 팀원들에게 지침을 주는 것으로, 고립과 반대되는 개념이다. ②는 개인적 목표 설정으로 본문의 고립과 직접 연결되지 않는다. ③은 주의 산만을 피하기 위한 기술 향상으로 본문의 의미와 다르다. ④는 성공에만 집중하는 태도로 벽을 쌓는 것과는 다른 차원의 설명이다.

4) [정답] ①
해설
a horizon of his own은 문맥상 각 개인이 자신의 욕구와 기대 수준을 결정하는 고유한 한계나 범위를 의미한다. 지문에서는 사람마다 원하는 것과 그것을 얻을 수 있다고 생각하는 범위가 다르며, 이로 인해 행복이나 만족감이 달라진다고 설명하고 있다. 따라서 a personal limit to his desires and expectations(자신의 욕구와 기대의 개인적 한계)이 가장 적절한 해석이다.
②는 재산의 총액 계산으로 본문의 의미와 다르다. ③은 문화

적 배경과의 연결로, 지문에서는 언급되지 않은 요소이다. ④는 재정적 독립과 관련된 표현으로, 본문의 욕구와 기대의 한계라는 맥락과 맞지 않는다. ⑤는 타인과의 비교 경향으로, 지문은 자기 기준에 따른 기대치에 초점을 두고 있다.

5) [정답] ④
해설
the language of smell은 문맥상 꽃들이 동물들을 유인하기 위해 사용하는 향기의 기능적 역할을 비유적으로 표현한 것이다. 즉, 네온사인이나 글자 대신 향기를 통해 잠재적 방문자(동물)를 끌어들이는 커뮤니케이션 수단이라는 의미다. 따라서 a means of communication using scents to attract visitors(향기를 사용하여 방문자를 끌어들이는 의사소통 수단)가 가장 적절한 해석이다.
①은 색깔 패턴을 통한 전달로 "향기(language of smell)"와는 다르다. ②는 포식자 경고 신호로 본문과 관련 없다. ③은 신체적 접촉으로 유발되는 본능적 행동으로, 향기를 통한 유인이라는 맥락과 맞지 않는다. ⑤는 종 간 먹이섭취를 막는 유전적 적응으로 본문 내용과 일치하지 않는다.

6) [정답] ②
해설
emotional interest rate는 문맥상 보상이 가까워질수록 사람들이 즉각적인 보상에 더 높은 가치를 부여하게 되는 심리적 경향을 뜻한다. 이는 hyperbolic discounting이라는 현상과 연결되어 즉각적인 보상이 주는 유혹이 커지며, 이를 위해 미래의 더 큰 보상을 포기하게 되는 현상을 설명한다. 따라서 the increased value people place on immediate rewards(사람들이 즉각적인 보상에 더 높은 가치를 두는 것)가 가장 적절한 해석이다.
①은 시장 조건에 따른 투자 수익률로, 심리적 반응과는 관련 없다. ③은 만족 지연의 재무적 비용으로 본문에서 설명하는 감정적 반응과는 다르다. ④는 논리적 계산으로 본문에서는 오히려 감정에 의해 비논리적 결정이 이루어짐을 강조한다. ⑤는 물가 상승률로 본문의 심리적 가치 변화와는 무관하다.

7) [정답] ⑤
해설
it is actually determined는 문맥상 아이의 왼손잡이나 오른손잡이 여부가 발달 과정에서 어느 시점에 생물학적으로 결정되는지에 관한 질문과 연결되어 있다. 이는 기존의 생각과 달리 초등학교 시기보다 훨씬 이른 시점, 심지어 태아 시기에 이미 선호가 나타난다는 연구 결과와도 일치한다. 따라서 it is biologically established at a specific point in development(발달 과정의 특정 시점에서 생물학적으로 결정된다)가 가장 적절한 해석이다.
①은 반복 훈련을 통한 학습으로 본문과 다르다. ②는 주로 문화적 영향에 의존한다는 설명이지만, 본문은 생물학적 근거를 강조한다. ③은 평생 완전히 무작위라는 내용과는 반대이다. ④는 언어 표현과 관련되지만 본문에서는 운동 선호가 태아 단계에서 나타난다고 말한다.

8) [정답] ③
해설
the reverse was true는 문맥상 "US dairy product imports in Mexico decreased from 2019 to 2020"라는 문장 바로 뒤에서 다른 세 나라에서는 반대의 변화, 즉 수입이 감소한 것이 아니라 증가했음을 설명하기 위해 사용되었다. 따라서 imports increased instead of decreased(수입이

감소한 것이 아니라 증가했다)가 가장 적절한 해석이다.
①은 변화가 없는 경우로 reverse(반대)를 충분히 설명하지 못한다. ②는 예측 불가능한 변동을 의미하지만 본문은 명확한 증가를 말하고 있다. ④는 빠른 감소를 뜻하지만 여기서는 증가가 반대 의미로 등장한다. ⑤는 시장 동향과 무관함을 의미하지만 본문은 수입 증가라는 명확한 변화를 강조한다.

9) [정답] ②
해설
strengthened his reputation는 문맥상 브루넬레스키가 여러 훌륭한 건축 작품을 통해 사람들 사이에서 그의 명성이 더욱 높아졌음을 의미한다. 즉, 그의 건축적 업적이 쌓이면서 타인의 평가와 존경이 증가했음을 나타낸다. 따라서 enhanced how highly he was regarded by others(그가 다른 사람들에게 얼마나 높이 평가받았는지를 높여 주었다)가 가장 적절한 해석이다.
①은 여행 기회를 언급하나 본문에서는 명성과 관련된 영향을 말하고 있다. ③은 건축 양식의 변화를 뜻하나 본문에서는 그러한 내용이 없다. ④는 동료들과의 불화를 언급하지만 본문에서는 긍정적인 평가와 성공을 강조한다. ⑤는 다른 분야에서 일할 수 있는 능력의 제한을 말하나 본문과 관련이 없다.

10) [정답] ④
해설
stick with it는 문맥상 관찰 시에 정한 관점(viewpoint)을 일관되게 유지해야 한다는 의미로 사용되었다. 이는 관점이 바뀌면 그에 따라 원근법에 표현되는 깊이와 형태가 달라지기 때문에 일정한 시점에서 계속해서 대상을 관찰하고 그에 맞게 그려야 한다는 뜻이다. 따라서 maintain a consistent point of observation(일관된 관찰 지점을 유지하다)가 가장 적절한 해석이다.
①은 다양한 각도에서 관찰하는 것을 의미하지만 여기서는 한 관점을 고수하는 것을 강조한다. ②는 더 나은 디테일을 위해 시점을 바꾸는 것으로 stick with it과 반대 의미이다. ③도 시점을 자주 바꾸는 것을 뜻하며 본문의 취지와 다르다. ⑤는 기하학적 규칙을 엄격히 따르는 것을 강조하지만 stick with it은 관점 유지에 관한 표현이다.

11) [정답] ①
해설
this notion은 문맥상 석유 가격 상승이 경제 전반에 부정적인 영향을 준다는 생각을 가리킨다. 이는 바로 앞 문장인 sudden rise in oil prices is never good news라는 내용과 연결되며, 역사적 사례와 경제 연구 결과가 이를 뒷받침한다고 설명하고 있다. 따라서 the idea that a rise in oil prices negatively affects the economy(석유 가격 상승이 경제에 부정적 영향을 준다는 생각)가 가장 적절한 해석이다.
②는 예측의 어려움에 대한 내용으로 본문에서 강조된 바 없다. ③은 장기적 영향이 없다는 가정으로 본문의 입장과 반대된다. ④는 에너지 부문 성장의 보편적 이익을 주장하지만 본문에서는 일반 경제에 부정적 영향을 강조한다. ⑤는 석유 생산 수준 유지에 관한 의견으로 언급되지 않았다.

12) [정답] ⑤
해설
wakes up the self는 문맥상 자신과 관련이 있다고 느끼게 만들어 정보를 더 강하게 인식하게 한다는 의미로 사용되었

다. 이는 단순한 숫자(33%)보다는 구체적이고 개인적으로 와닿는 표현("당신 옆의 두 사람 중 한 명이 내년에 없을 것이다")이 개인적인 반응과 관심을 불러일으킨다는 점을 강조한다. 따라서 makes students personally relate to the information(학생들이 그 정보를 개인적으로 연결 지어 생각하게 한다)가 가장 적절한 해석이다.
①, ②, ③, ④는 모두 학습 전략, 생활 습관, 조언 요청과 관련된 내용으로 본문의 핵심인 개인적 관련성 자극과는 거리가 있다.

13) [정답] ③
해설
win over the masses는 문맥상 일반 대중이 새로운 가상 기술(컴퓨터 기반 작업 환경)을 받아들이도록 설득하다는 의미로 사용되었다. Steve Jobs가 사람들이 익숙한 사무 환경과 새로운 가상 환경 사이에 유사성을 강조하는 비유를 통해 기술 수용을 촉진한 맥락과 연결된다. 따라서 gain the acceptance of ordinary people(일반 대중의 수용을 얻다)가 가장 적절한 해석이다.
①은 전문가를 대상으로 하는 설명으로 대중과는 다르다. ②는 기업 간 경쟁 유도로 본문과 관련 없다. ④는 회의적 사용자들의 비판 회피로 본문의 적극적 수용 유도와는 차이가 있다. ⑤는 정부 지원 확보로 본문의 대중 설득과 무관하다.

14) [정답] ④
해설
being blinded by modern lights는 문맥상 거북이들의 본능적 방향 감각이 인공적인 빛(해변의 인공조명)에 의해 방해받아 잘못된 방향으로 가게 되는 현상을 의미한다. 이는 본래 자연 환경에서 유효했던 진화적 전략이 현대 인공 환경에서는 잘못된 결과를 초래하게 되는 상황을 설명하는 표현이다. 따라서 having their natural behavior disrupted by artificial factors(자연스러운 행동이 인공적 요인에 의해 방해받는다)가 가장 적절한 해석이다.
①은 새로운 먹이원 적응으로 본문과 관련 없다. ②는 낯선 환경 회피로 본문에 언급되지 않았다. ③은 인간의 안내에 의존하는 내용으로 본문의 상황과 맞지 않는다. ⑤는 빛에 대한 민감성 증가로 본문의 의미와 다르다.

15) [정답] ⑤
해설
this concept는 문맥상 아리스토텔레스의 말인 "Nothing is in the mind that does not pass through the senses"를 가리킨다. 이는 인간의 마음(지식과 사고 포함)이 감각을 통해 들어오는 정보에 의존한다는 개념을 의미한다. 이후 실험 예시(감각 차단 시 사고 혼란과 환각 발생)는 바로 이 개념을 뒷받침한다. 따라서 all knowledge must enter the mind through the senses(모든 지식은 감각을 통해 마음에 들어온다)가 가장 적절한 해석이다.
①은 노력 없는 신체 기능 조절로 본문의 주제와 맞지 않는다. ②는 감각 차단의 장기적 건강 효과로 본문에서는 다루지 않았다. ③은 따뜻한 물 환경이 환각의 원인이라는 잘못된 해석이다. ④는 정보 저장량과 관련된 내용으로 본문의 핵심 개념과 다르다.

16) [정답] ①
해설
hardwired는 문맥상 다리와 발의 반응이 선천적이며 본능적으로 깊이 자리 잡혀 자동적으로 나타난다는 의미로 사용되었

다. 이는 수백만 년 동안 생존 반응으로 발달해왔으며 오늘날에도 여전히 의식적 사고 없이 즉각적으로 발휘되는 특성임을 강조한다. 따라서 firmly programmed into our natural behavior(우리의 자연스러운 행동에 단단히 내재된 것)가 가장 적절한 해석이다.

②는 사회적 기대에 의해 쉽게 영향을 받는다는 의미로 본문의 본능적, 자동적 반응과 반대이다. ③은 의식적 훈련으로 점진적 약화라는 의미로, 본문에서는 이러한 반응이 여전히 강하게 유지되고 있음을 강조한다. ④는 빠르게 환경에 적응한다는 뜻으로 본문의 hardwired 개념(이미 깊이 내재됨)과 맞지 않는다. ⑤는 외부 보상에 의해 주로 통제된다는 뜻으로 본문의 생존 본능적 반응 설명과 일치하지 않는다.

17) [정답] ③
해설
won out는 문맥상 종이가 다른 재료들(돌, 점토, 나무, 벽화 등)에 비해 더 적합하고 성공적인 선택지로 자리 잡았다는 의미로 사용되었다. 종이가 운반과 보존의 용이성 등 여러 장점을 통해 문자 기록의 주된 매체로 자리매김한 것을 설명한다. 따라서 became the preferred and most successful option(가장 선호되고 성공적인 선택지가 되었다)가 가장 적절한 해석이다.

①은 새로운 재료로 대체되었다는 뜻으로 본문의 취지와 다르다. ②는 특정 지역에만 보존되었다는 의미로 전 세계적으로 퍼진 종이의 성공과 맞지 않는다. ④는 현대 기술에 맞게 수정되었다는 의미인데 본문에서는 종이의 초기 성공과 지속성을 강조한다. ⑤는 역사적 관심으로만 보관된다는 뜻으로 현재도 널리 사용되고 있는 종이의 역할과 어긋난다.

18) [정답] ②
해설
working through the connections는 문맥상 하나의 주장이나 이유가 여러 개념과 함의를 포함하고 있기 때문에, 그 아이디어들 사이의 관계를 면밀히 분석하고 논리적 연결을 명확히 해야 한다는 의미로 사용되었다. 이는 reasoning(추론)의 목적과도 일치하며, 결론과 이유 사이의 '명백해 보이는' 연결을 당연시하지 않고 철저히 논리적으로 검토해야 한다는 취지다. 따라서 carefully analyzing how different ideas relate to each other(서로 다른 아이디어들이 어떻게 관련되는지 면밀히 분석한다)가 가장 적절한 해석이다.

①은 감정적 호소 분석으로 본문과 관련이 없다. ③은 설득력을 높이기 위한 문장 수정으로 본문에서는 논리적 분석을 강조한다. ④는 관련 없는 주장에 새로운 증거를 추가하는 것으로 본문의 내용과 다르다. ⑤는 기억하기 쉽게 단순화하는 것인데, 본문은 오히려 복잡한 논리적 연결을 면밀히 검토해야 한다고 강조한다.

19) [정답] ⑤
해설
selective of persons는 문맥상 이주가 아무나가 아니라 특정한 특성을 가진 사람들(더 젊고, 건강하고, 유연하며, 더 나은 삶을 희망하는 이들)에게 주로 발생한다는 의미로 사용되었다. 즉, 이주는 자연스럽게 어떤 유리한 특성을 지닌 사람들을 주로 포함하게 되는 경향이 있다는 것이다. 따라서 involving mainly people with certain advantageous traits(주로 특정한 유리한 특성을 가진 사람들이 포함된다)가 가장 적절한 해석이다.

①은 노년층을 단념시키는 내용으로 본문의 핵심과 다르다. ②는 고학력자만 허용하는 정책적 제한으로 본문에 언급되지

않았다. ③은 가족 단위 이주를 권장한다는 내용인데 본문에서는 개인적 특성 중심의 선택성을 강조한다. ④는 정책적 제한 강화로 본문의 자연적 선택 경향과 맞지 않는다.

20) [정답] ③
해설
depriving governments of the power는 문맥상 정부가 화폐 공급을 과도하게 확대하여 인플레이션을 유발하는 것을 막기 위한 방법으로 금과 같은 공급이 제한된 자산을 화폐로 사용하는 것을 설명한다. 즉, 정부가 지나치게 많은 돈을 찍어내는 능력을 제한한다는 뜻이다. 따라서 limiting governments' ability to print excessive money(정부가 과도하게 화폐를 발행하는 능력을 제한한다)가 가장 적절한 해석이다.

①은 금리가 아니라 화폐 발행 능력에 대한 논의이다. ②는 금의 가치 통제에 대한 내용으로 본문에서는 화폐 공급 통제가 핵심이다. ④는 국제 무역 촉진과 관련 없으며, ⑤는 세금 수입 증가에 관한 내용도 본문에서 언급되지 않는다.

21) [정답] ①
해설
"This"가 지칭하는 내용은 감정 중추 손상이 판단력을 떨어뜨린다는 연구 결과이다. 이는 감정을 이성의 방해물로만 간주했던 전통 경제학 이론과 정면으로 충돌한다는 점에서, 핵심 함축 의미는 '감정이 오히려 의사결정에 필요하다'는 것이다. 따라서 정답은 ①번이다.

②번은 감정과 이성을 분리해야 한다는 잘못된 가정을 반복하고 있고, ③번은 기존 경제학 이론을 왜곡한 주장이다. ④, ⑤번 역시 지문과 정반대되는 내용을 담고 있다.

22) [정답] ④
해설
tyranny of choice는 문맥상 선택지가 많을수록 자유가 아니라 오히려 결정을 어렵게 만들고 스트레스를 유발한다는 심리적 현상을 의미한다. 이는 사람들이 많은 비교를 해야 하고, 잘못된 결정을 할까 봐 걱정하며, 결정 후에도 후회하는 경향으로 이어진다. 따라서 a condition where having too many options makes decision-making harder(선택지가 너무 많아져서 결정이 더 어려워지는 상태)가 가장 적절한 해석이다.

①은 외부 요인에 의해 선택지가 제한되는 상황으로 본문과 다르다. ②는 보상을 늘려 동기를 부여하는 방법으로 본문의 선택의 부정적 영향과 관련 없다. ③은 전문가만이 결정을 내리는 체계로 본문의 일반 소비자의 선택 상황과 맞지 않는다. ⑤는 모든 선택이 동일한 결과를 낳는다는 의미로 본문의 선택 간 비교와 후회와는 다르다.

23) [정답] ①
해설
feeling the urgency of the situation는 문맥상 노인이 갑자기 넘어져 응급 상황이 발생했음을 인식하고 신속하게 대응할 필요성을 느꼈다는 의미로 사용되었다. Linda가 잠시 얼어붙었다가 바로 무릎을 꿇고 노인 곁으로 다가가는 행동에서 이를 확인할 수 있다. 따라서 realizing that immediate action was needed(즉각적인 행동이 필요하다는 것을 인식하다)가 가장 적절한 해석이다.

②는 다른 승객들의 반응을 걱정하는 내용으로 본문과 맞지 않는다. ③은 전문가가 올 때까지 기다리는 결정을 뜻하지만 Linda는 바로 행동에 나섰다. ④는 기차가 갑자기 멈춘 것을 알아챘다는 내용인데 본문에서는 그런 언급이 없다. ⑤

Answer Keys

는 가방을 더 일찍 도와주지 못한 것을 후회한다는 내용인데 urgency는 현재 상황의 긴박감과 관련된다.

1) [정답] ⑤
[요약문] Exceptional teaching improved students' Spanish skills, so contract renewal is offered for next year.

2) [정답] ④
[요약문] Peter's daughter had a sudden fever, got treated at the hospital, and recovered by night.

3) [정답] ①
[요약문] Good leaders stay connected like porous teabags, allowing interaction with people and community.

4) [정답] ①
[요약문] Desire for wealth is endless because expectations constantly rise, making satisfaction relative and unreachable.

5) [정답] ③
[요약문] Flowers attract animals like restaurants attract customers, using scents instead of words to advertise.

6) [정답] ③
[요약문] Larger delayed rewards are often chosen over sooner ones, except when immediate reward is available now.

7) [정답] ④
[요약문] Handedness develops before birth, as unborn babies show early preference for right-hand movement.

8) [정답] ②
[요약문] Mexico consistently imported most US dairy, but others saw increase while Mexico's imports decreased.

9) [정답] ⑤
[요약문] Brunelleschi, trained as goldsmith, became Renaissance architect and designed Florence's famous

10) [정답] ③
[요약문] Youth Leaders Camp offers teens workshops, tours, and leadership projects over three days in Canada.

11) [정답] ⑤
[요약문] Plogging event encourages eco-friendly jogging by picking up trash around Lake Union in September.

12) [정답] ①
[요약문] To draw realistic depth, artists observe shapes and stick to a consistent viewpoint when drawing.

13) [정답] ③

[요약문] Low oil prices reduce production costs and stimulate economy, while price hikes shrink GDP growth.

14) [정답] ④
[요약문] We better remember self-related info because it links to strong personal associations in the brain.

15) [정답] ⑤
[요약문] Steve Jobs used analogy to connect physical office tools to virtual ones for easier tech adoption.

16) [정답] ②
[요약문] Baby turtles once followed moonlight to sea, but now follow artificial lights leading to danger.

17) [정답] ②
[요약문] Brain alone cannot sense because sensory input through organs is essential for awareness and thought.

18) [정답] ④
[요약문] Feet reflect emotions instinctively, as evolutionary responses remain strong in modern behavior.

19) [정답] ③
[요약문] Paper and codex revolutionized writing, replacing heavy, fragile, and immobile earlier materials.

20) [정답] ④
[요약문] Good reasoning breaks a conclusion into precise premises instead of relying on one vague claim.

21) [정답] ②
[요약문] Migration is often voluntary and beneficial, redistributing labor and improving opportunities.

22) [정답] ③
[요약문] Gold-backed money limits inflation since governments can't easily overproduce a rare resource.

23) [정답] ①
[요약문] Emotions help decision making by working with reason, challenging purely rational economic models.

24) [정답] ⑤
[요약문] Too many choices increase stress and regret, making people less satisfied despite more freedom.

25) [정답] ⑤
[요약문] Linda helped a fainting elderly woman on train, realizing even uncertain small actions matter.

1) ⑤

해설
①은 학년 간 비교를 다루지 않고 있어 글의 주제와 맞지 않습

니다.
②는 외국어 학습의 중요성을 언급하고 있지 않아 적절하지 않습니다.
③은 학생들의 자신감을 향상시키는 전략에 초점을 맞추고 있지만, 이는 글의 중심 내용이 아닙니다.
④는 스페인어 교수법에 대한 평가가 아니라 Ms. Lopez의 기여에 대한 감사와 계약 연장이 중심이므로 부적절합니다.
⑤는 Ms. Lopez에게 계약 연장을 제안하는 내용을 정확히 포괄하고 있어 정답입니다.

2) ②
해설
①은 병원 직원에 대한 신뢰를 언급하지만, 지문의 중심 감정은 '안도감'에 있습니다.
②는 자녀가 아플 때 병원 치료를 받고 안도하게 되는 아버지의 감정을 정확히 반영하고 있어 정답입니다.
③은 가족 일상의 변화에 초점을 두고 있어 지엽적입니다.
④는 증상의 조기 인식보다는 치료 후 변화가 중심 내용이므로 적절하지 않습니다.
⑤는 야간 소아 진료의 가치를 말하지만, 시간대는 맥락적 배경일 뿐 핵심 논지가 아닙니다.

3) ①
해설
①은 차와 물의 비유를 통해 강조된 리더의 개방성과 연결의 중요성을 정확히 반영하고 있어 정답입니다.
②는 의사소통 경로에 관한 언급은 있지만, 핵심 논지는 '다른 사람과의 연결'입니다.
③은 좋은 자원의 중요성에 초점을 맞추지만, 글의 주제는 개방성과 관계 형성입니다.
④는 조직의 성공에 있어 일관성의 역할을 다루지 않으므로 부적절합니다.
⑤는 독립성의 장점을 말하지만, 본문은 오히려 고립을 경계하고 협력을 강조합니다.

4) ②
해설:
①은 사회적 지위에 대한 언급이 없어 부적절합니다.
②는 인간의 부에 대한 만족이 절대적인 양이 아니라 기대와 비교한 상대적인 기준에 따라 달라진다는 글의 핵심 논지를 잘 반영하여 정답입니다.
③은 합리적인 재정 목표 설정의 필요성을 강조하지 않으므로 주제가 아닙니다.
④는 과도한 소비의 위험성에 초점을 맞추고 있지 않아 적절하지 않습니다.
⑤는 도덕적 가치와 부의 차이를 논하지 않기 때문에 주제에서 벗어납니다.

5) ②
해설:

①은 꽃들이 향기를 이용해 동물을 유인하는 자연의 마케팅 전략을 설명하므로 정답입니다.
②의 내용은 도입부에서 꽃의 전략을 설명하기 위한 비유일 뿐, 지문의 주제가 아닙니다.
③은 시각적 광고의 발전을 다루지 않으며, 글은 오히려 시각 대신 후각적 표현을 강조합니다.
④는 인간의 문자 언어 자체를 주제로 한 것이 아니므로 적절하지 않습니다.
⑤는 영양 보상 자체보다는 유인을 위한 전략에 중점을 두고 있어 부적절합니다.

6) ③
해설
①은 지연된 만족의 이점을 설명하지만, 지문은 인간이 어떻게 그 이점을 놓치는지를 설명합니다.
②는 감정적 투자와 재정적 투자의 비교를 다루고 있지 않으므로 적절하지 않습니다.
③은 즉각적인 보상이 등장할 때 인간의 선택이 어떻게 달라지는지를 설명하므로, 지문의 주제에 적합합니다.
④는 일관된 선택의 중요성을 강조하지만, 주된 초점은 시간 지연에 따른 판단 변화입니다.
⑤는 투자에서의 위험 인식보다는 보상 시점에 따른 심리적 반응에 중점을 두고 있어 부적절합니다.

7) ④
해설
①은 교육의 영향에 초점을 두고 있으나, 글은 생물학적 기원을 다룹니다.
②는 아동과 성인의 운동 능력 비교가 주제가 아니므로 적절하지 않습니다.
③은 쓰기 활동을 통한 손잡이 판단 시점에 대한 옛 견해일 뿐, 글의 핵심은 아닙니다.
④는 손잡이 성향이 초등학교 이전, 심지어 태아기부터 나타난다는 연구 결과를 중심으로 전개된 글의 주제와 정확히 일치하여 정답입니다.
⑤는 초음파 데이터 해석의 어려움을 다루지 않으므로 주제에서 벗어납니다.

8) ⑤
해설
①은 전 세계 유제품 소비율 비교를 다루지 않으므로 부적절합니다.
②는 멕시코의 감소 원인에 대한 분석이 아니기 때문에 주제가 아닙니다.
③은 무역 정책의 역할을 언급하지 않으므로 적절하지 않습니다.
④는 인구 증가의 영향을 다룬 내용이 없어 주제에서 벗어납니다.
⑤는 미국 유제품 수출이 국가별로 2018~2020년 동안 어떤

추세를 보였는지 설명한 지문과 가장 잘 부합하여 정답입니다.

9) ①
해설
①은 브루넬레스키의 생애와 업적, 특히 르네상스 건축에 끼친 영향 전반을 다룬 지문 내용과 정확히 일치하여 정답입니다.
②는 도나텔로에 대한 언급은 있으나 주된 초점은 브루넬레스키에 있으므로 부적절합니다.
③은 고딕과 르네상스 건축 비교를 다루지 않으므로 적절하지 않습니다.
④는 일 두오모의 돔은 언급되지만, 그 상징성 분석은 지문의 주제가 아닙니다.
⑤는 로마 유적이 언급되지만, 이는 브루넬레스키의 학습 배경일 뿐 주제가 아닙니다.

10) ①
해설:
①은 청소년 리더십 캠프에 대한 소개와 등록 정보를 제공하는 지문의 내용을 정확히 반영하여 정답입니다.
②는 항공권 예약 서비스에 대한 정보가 아니므로 적절하지 않습니다.
③은 대학의 리더십 과정 비교가 아니라 캠프 소개이므로 부적절합니다.
④는 문화 교류 장학금 안내가 아니므로 해당되지 않습니다.
⑤는 과거 프로그램의 평가가 아니라 향후 일정 공지이므로 주제가 아닙니다.

11) ②
해설
①은 행사 조직 요령을 다루지 않으므로 부적절합니다.
②는 지역 사회에서 환경 보호를 위한 달리기와 쓰레기 줍기 행사 공지를 주제로 한 지문의 내용과 정확히 일치하여 정답입니다.
③은 호수 생태계 소개가 아니므로 주제가 아닙니다.
④는 마라톤 훈련 지침과 무관합니다.
⑤는 환경 오염 보고가 아니라 환경 보호 활동 안내이므로 적절하지 않습니다.

12) ③
해설:
①은 추상과 사실적 표현의 비교가 주제가 아닙니다.
②는 빛과 그림자는 지문의 부차적 요소이므로, 지문의 주제에 적합하지 않습니다.
③은 예술에서 원근법을 이용해 깊이와 입체감을 표현하는 다양한 기술과 관찰의 중요성을 설명한 지문과 잘 맞아 정답입니다.
④는 르네상스 시대의 기하학 원리 역사에 대한 내용이 없으므로 부적절합니다.
⑤는 색상 없이 사실적인 그림을 그리는 어려움이 아니라, 원근 표현의 원리를 설명하고 있습니다.

13) ④
해설:
①은 석유의 생산과 소비 역사에 대한 설명이 아니므로 부적절합니다.
②는 에너지 산업 투자 장점이 아닌, 석유 가격 변동이 전체 경제에 미치는 영향을 다룹니다.
③은 화석 연료 의존의 위험을 언급하지 않으므로 적절하지 않습니다.
④는 석유 가격의 상승과 하락이 산업 비용, GDP, 경제 성장에 어떤 영향을 미치는지를 다룬 지문과 정확히 일치하여 정답입니다.
⑤는 물류 산업과 자동차 산업의 차이를 중심으로 다루지 않아 주제가 아닙니다.

14) ①
해설
①은 정보가 자아와 관련될 때 더 잘 기억되고 이해된다는 지문의 핵심 논지를 잘 반영하여 정답입니다.
②는 생소한 상황에서 기억이 약해지는 이유를 언급하지만, 주된 논지는 자아 관련성입니다.
③은 통계 정보의 감정적 영향에 초점을 맞추고 있으나, 글은 자아에 관련된 정보의 효과를 강조합니다.
④는 학업 성공에서의 또래 영향이 아니라 자아 중심 처리에 대한 설명이므로 부적절합니다.
⑤는 청소년기의 자기 인식 어려움을 다루지 않으며, 본문은 자아의 정보 처리 능력을 강조합니다.

15) ⑤
해설
①은 디자인 미학의 영향보다는 용어의 유사성을 통한 이해 촉진이 중심이므로 주제가 아닙니다.
②는 애플과 다른 기술 회사의 비교를 다루지 않으므로 적절하지 않습니다.
③은 가상 사무실이 생산성에 미친 영향이 아니라, 기술 수용 과정에서의 유추 사용에 초점이 맞춰져 있습니다.
④는 커뮤니케이션 방식의 역사적 변화를 다루지 않으며 부적절합니다.
⑤는 스티브 잡스가 새로운 기술을 이해시키기 위해 기존에 익숙한 개념과의 유사점을 활용했다는 지문의 중심 내용을 정확히 반영하여 정답입니다.

16) ④
해설:
④는 바다거북이 조상으로부터 이어받은 생존 전략이 현대 환경에서는 오히려 해가 된다는 지문의 핵심 논지를 잘 반영하여 정답입니다.
②는 동물의 빛 감지 능력 자체의 이점을 강조하고 있으나, 글의 주제는 진화한 본능이 현대 환경과 충돌하는 문제입니다.
③은 해안 개발이 관광에 미치는 영향을 다루지 않으므로 부적

절합니다.
①은 종 간 행동 비교가 아니며, 바다거북 일반에 대한 설명입니다.
⑤는 달 주기보다는 인공 조명이 가져온 변화가 중심이므로 주제가 아닙니다.

17)
해설:
①은 종 간 감각 기능 비교가 아니므로 적절하지 않습니다.
②는 아리스토텔레스의 철학은 인용되었지만, 지문의 중심은 철학사적 논의가 아닙니다.
③은 뇌가 외부 세계와 연결되기 위해 감각 기관에 의존하며, 이 감각 입력이 사고와 성격 등 정신 기능에 필수적이라는 글의 핵심 내용을 정확히 반영하여 정답입니다.
④는 뇌수술 기술의 발전은 보조적 설명일 뿐 주제가 아닙니다.
⑤는 감각 차단의 신체적 위험보다는 정신 기능과의 관계를 중심으로 하고 있으므로 부적절합니다.

18) ③
해설
①은 걷기와 달리기 기술의 발달에 대한 내용이 아니며, 생존 본능에 초점을 둡니다.
②는 언어적 의사소통보다는 비언어적 반응에 초점이 있으므로 부적절합니다.
③은 다리와 발의 움직임이 감정과 생각을 솔직하게 드러내며, 그 반응이 진화적 생존 본능에 기반한다는 글의 핵심 내용을 정확히 반영하여 정답입니다.
④는 자세보다는 다리와 발의 반응을 다루므로 주제가 아닙니다.
⑤는 전체 몸짓 언어 해석보다는 다리와 발의 표현에 집중하므로 적절하지 않습니다.

19) ⑤
해설
①은 초기 기록 기술의 환경적 영향을 설명하지만, 이는 지문의 주제가 아닙니다.
②는 현대 교육에서의 구술 전통 감소를 다루지 않으며, 지문의 시점은 주로 과거입니다.
③은 로마의 발명이 중국 문화에 끼친 영향을 설명하지 않으므로 부적절합니다.
④는 고대 사회의 스토리텔링 방법 비교가 아닌, 기록 매체의 발전이 중심입니다.
⑤는 지식 전달 방식이 구술에서 문자로 전환되는 과정에서 다양한 필기 재료들이 사용되었고, 종이가 궁극적으로 승자가 되었다는 지문의 핵심 내용을 정확히 반영하여 정답입니다.

20) ①
해설
①은 결론에 도달하기 위한 이유가 단일한 주장으로 이루어지기 어렵고, 복잡한 사고 과정을 분석해야 한다는 글의 핵심 논지를 정확히 포괄합니다.
②는 교육이 경제에 미치는 영향을 강조하지만, 이는 예시의 일부일 뿐 글의 주제는 아닙니다.
③은 예시로 제시된 주장이지 글의 중심 내용은 아닙니다.
④는 정책과 고등교육 간의 관계를 언급하지만, 글의 주요 논의는 추론 과정의 복잡성에 있습니다.
⑤는 잘 교육된 인구의 중요성을 강조하나, 이는 글의 중심이 아닌 부수적인 내용입니다.

21) ②
해설
①은 도시 과밀 문제의 원인을 다루지 않으며 지문의 주요 논점과 맞지 않습니다.
②는 일반적으로 부정적으로 인식되는 이주 현상에 대해 보다 균형 잡힌 관점을 제시하며, 이주가 문제뿐만 아니라 해결책이 될 수 있음을 강조하는 지문의 핵심 내용을 잘 반영하여 정답입니다.
③은 이주민의 의료 문제에 대한 내용이 언급되지 않아 적절하지 않습니다.
④는 국제 정치와의 관련성은 지문에서 다루지 않으므로 부적절합니다.
⑤는 이주의 역사적 양상을 설명하지 않으므로 주제가 아닙니다.

22) ③
해설
①은 무역에 대한 언급이 없으므로 부적절합니다.
②는 제한된 자원을 화폐로 사용할 때의 위험을 강조하고 있지 않으므로 적절하지 않습니다.
③은 금이 공급 제한을 통해 화폐 발행을 억제하고 인플레이션을 방지하는 수단으로 기능한다는 지문의 핵심 논지를 정확히 반영하여 정답입니다.
④는 고대와 현대의 은행 제도를 비교하지 않으므로 주제가 아닙니다.
⑤는 정부 지출이 신뢰에 미치는 영향을 다루지 않아 부적절합니다.

23) ⑤
해설
①은 신경과학이 경제 예측에 미치는 영향을 설명하지만, 지문에서 다루지 않은 내용이므로 주제가 아닙니다.
②는 전통 경제 이론의 한계가 언급되지만, 보조적 내용일 뿐 중심 주제는 아닙니다.
③은 감정 조절보다는 의사결정의 질에 영향을 주는 감정의 역할이 핵심이므로 부적절합니다.
④는 인지와 기억의 관계가 아니라 감정과 의사결정의 관계가 중심이므로 적절하지 않습니다.
⑤는 감정이 의사결정 과정에서 부정적 요소가 아니라 오히려

중요한 긍정적 역할을 한다는 연구 결과를 중심으로 전개된 지문의 핵심 내용을 정확히 반영하여 정답입니다.

24) ④
해설
①은 후회 방지 전략을 이야기하지만, 지문은 선택 자체가 후회를 유발한다는 주장을 다룹니다.
②는 명확한 선호의 중요성을 언급하지 않으며, 선택 폭의 문제가 주제입니다.
③은 문화 간 의사결정 방식의 비교가 아닌, 일반적인 인간 심리에 관한 설명입니다.
④는 선택의 폭이 넓어질수록 사람들이 스트레스를 받고 불행해질 수 있다는 '선택의 역설'을 중심으로 전개된 지문의 핵심 논지를 정확히 반영하여 정답입니다.
⑤는 직원 만족에 대한 유인책은 사례로 언급되었을 뿐, 지문의 중심 주제가 아닙니다.

25) ⑤
해설
①은어린 시절 기억과 현재 선택의 관계는 지문에서 다루지 않으므로 부적절합니다.
②는 철도 안전이 지문의 중심 주제가 아니며, 에피소드의 배경일 뿐입니다.
③은 저혈압에 대한 설명은 있지만 주제가 아니라, 상황의 원인일 뿐입니다.
④는 장거리 여행의 어려움에 관한 내용은 언급되지 않습니다.
⑤는 리다가 망설임 끝에 도움을 선택하고, 그 작은 행동이 의미 있는 결과를 가져오는 경험을 중심으로 전개된 지문의 핵심 내용을 정확히 반영하여 정답입니다.

1) ③
해설
①: 새로운 교수법 탐구 의지는 문맥상 긍정적이지만, 문장 전체의 흐름과 직접 연결되기 어렵습니다.
②: 학교의 커리큘럼 개발 강조는 Ms. Lopez 개인의 계약 연장과는 거리가 있습니다.
③: '계약 연장을 제안하며, 그 연장이 학생들의 학습 경험과 성취를 향상시킬 것'이라는 논리 흐름에 가장 적절한 표현입니다.
④: Ms. Lopez의 명성은 긍정적 정보이지만, '학생들의 학습 경험 향상'과 직접 연결되기 어렵습니다.
⑤: 감사 표현은 Ms. Lopez의 기여에 대한 결과이지만, 향후의 긍정적 영향에 대한 논리 연결은 약합니다.

2) ③
해설
①: 긴 밤을 보낸 것은 맞지만, 좌절의 감정을 느끼지 않았으므로 오답입니다.
②: 병원 방문 시점에 대한 후회는 지문 어디에도 언급되지 않습니다.
③: 딸이 평화롭게 자는 모습을 보며 느낀 'calm'이라는 단어

가 지문 마지막 문장에 직접 사용되었기 때문에, 가장 정확한 정답입니다.
④: 질병에 대한 초기 반응에 대한 후회는 지문에 나타나지 않습니다.
⑤: 열이 다시 날까 봐 불안해하는 감정은 마지막 문장의 'calm'과 상반되므로 문맥상 맞지 않습니다.

3) ③
해설
①: 아이디어를 외부 영향으로부터 보호해야 한다는 주장은 본문의 핵심 비유(소통과 연결)의 의미와 반대되는 방향입니다.
②: 권위와 거리를 강조하는 것은 리더가 벽을 쌓아선 안 된다는 본문의 메시지와 어긋납니다.
③: 'The tea was meant to mix with the water'에 이어지는 비유로, 사람들 또한 서로 연결되어야 한다는 본문의 핵심 주장을 그대로 이어가는 문장으로 정답입니다.
④: 개인 목표에만 집중하는 것은 '함께 일하고 연결되어야 한다'는 본문의 주장과 상반됩니다.
⑤: 리더는 거리감을 유지해야 한다는 내용은 본문의 핵심 내용과 일치하지 않아 오답입니다.

4) ③
해설
①: 기대가 많아질수록 불행해질 수 있다는 논지를 볼 때, 기대가 줄어든다는 내용은 문맥에 맞지 않습니다.
②: 목표 설정으로 욕망을 통제할 수 있다는 주장은 본문에서 '욕망에 한계를 두기 어렵다'는 주장과 상반됩니다.
③: 마지막 문장 "every man has a horizon of his own…"은 빈칸에 들어가야 할 결론 문장이며, 전체 지문의 논지를 자연스럽게 마무리해 줍니다.
④: 부의 가치는 물질적 필요 충족이라는 주장은 본문의 상대적 욕망과 기대의 개념과는 어긋납니다.
⑤: 소유에 따른 행복 기준이 고정되어 있다는 주장은 '행복은 기대와의 비율'이라는 본문 핵심 논지와 반대됩니다.

5) ④
해설
①: 외형 인식만으로 꽃을 알아본다는 내용은 본문에 언급되지 않습니다.
②: 꽃이 상업적 간판과 유사한 색을 낸다는 내용은 본문에서 언급된 '냄새' 중심 설명과 다릅니다.
③: 곤충이 학습을 통해 식물을 구분한다는 주장은 지문에 나타나지 않습니다.
④: 바로 앞 문장에서 "they advertise… using the language of smell"이라는 문장이 직접 제시되어, 빈칸에 가장 적절한 문장입니다.
⑤: 자연계가 무작위로 수분된다는 내용은 본문의 의도적 유인 구조에 반하며, 오답입니다.

6) ④

해설

①: 이자율 계산 능력 향상은 본문의 핵심 주제와 관련이 없습니다.

②: 적은 보상이 더 공정하게 느껴진다는 설명은 본문에 나타나지 않습니다.

③: 실제로는 즉시 받는 보상을 더 높게 평가하므로 오답입니다.

④: "The introduction of 'now' causes us to make inconsistent decisions"라는 문장이 지문의 핵심 주장을 직접 설명하며, 빈칸에 가장 적절한 문장입니다.

⑤: 기다릴수록 참을성이 생긴다는 설명은 본문의 두 사례를 비교하는 논리와 맞지 않으므로 오답입니다.

7) ③

해설

①: 아이들이 학교에서 손잡이를 바꾼다는 내용은 지문에 전혀 언급되지 않았으며, 논지와 맞지 않습니다.

②: 유전과 환경의 영향을 두고 연구자들이 확신하지 못한다는 내용은 지문에서 다뤄지지 않았습니다.

③: 태아 단계에서 85%가 오른팔을 더 많이 움직이며, 이는 성인의 약 89.4%가 오른손잡이라는 사실과 유사하므로, 손잡이의 발달이 매우 이른 시기에 결정된다는 본문의 핵심 주장과 일치하는 문장입니다.

④: 초음파 기술의 한계는 언급되지 않았으며, 본문의 과학적 연구 결과와도 관련이 없습니다.

⑤: 성인이 되면 손잡이 비율이 균등해진다는 주장은 본문의 정보와 정반대이며, 잘못된 내용입니다.

8) ④

해설

①: 중국에서 지속적인 증가가 아닌, 2018년에서 2019년 사이 감소가 있었으므로 오답입니다.

②: "China was the only country where imports of US dairy products dropped between 2018 and 2019."라는 문장이 지문에 명시되어 있어, 이 문장이 가장 자연스럽게 빈칸을 이어주는 문장이며 정답입니다.

③: 멕시코는 2019년에서 2020년 사이 수입이 감소했다고 언급되었으므로 오답입니다.

④: 필리핀에서 수입이 감소했다는 내용은 지문에 없으며, 오히려 증가한 것으로 보입니다.

⑤: 인도네시아는 2020년 수입이 2018년의 두 배 이상으로 증가했다고 되어 있으므로 오답입니다.

9) ②

해설

①: 조각가라는 표현은 지문에서 Donatello에게 해당되며, Brunelleschi는 건축가입니다.

②: "Filippo Brunelleschi is considered to be the founding father of Renaissance architecture."라는 문장을

그대로 반영한 표현으로 정답입니다.

③: 'the last artist'는 본문의 맥락과 전혀 맞지 않습니다.

④: 정신적 지도자라는 표현은 지문에 등장하지 않으며 관련이 없습니다.

⑤: 후원자(patron)는 예술가를 지원하는 인물로, Brunelleschi와는 다른 역할입니다.

10) ③

해설

①: 학문적 탐구를 장려하는 캠프는 본문의 리더십 중심 목적과 다릅니다.

②: 외국어 학습 관련 프로그램이라는 내용은 지문과 맞지 않습니다.

③: 지문 첫 문장에서 "to improve your leadership"이라는 문구가 직접 제시되어 있으며, 캠프 목적과 완벽하게 부합합니다.

④: 국제 스포츠 대회를 강조하는 캠프는 본문 내용과 관련이 없습니다.

⑤: 취업 기회를 제공하는 캠프가 아니라는 점에서 오답입니다.

11) ③

해설

①: 건강 관리 역시 행사와 관련 있지만, 본문 제목과 정확히 일치하지 않습니다.

②: 경치 감상은 지문에서 언급되지 않았고 핵심 메시지가 아닙니다.

③: 원문 제목 문구 "conserve the Earth"를 그대로 반영한 표현으로, 쓰레기를 줍는 활동의 목적과 가장 잘 맞습니다.

④: 경쟁 요소는 지문 어디에도 언급되지 않아 부적절한 선택입니다.

⑤: 체력 테스트 준비라는 표현은 본문의 활동 취지와 맞지 않으므로 오답입니다.

12) ③

해설

①: 재료의 차이에 따른 깊이 표현은 본문에서 언급되지 않았습니다.

②: 단순화된 이미지에 대한 선호는 본문의 내용과 무관합니다.

③: 바로 다음 문장 "Because of this, it's important to establish the viewpoint…"과 자연스럽게 연결되며, 시각 위치에 따라 사물이 다르게 보인다는 내용은 빈칸에 가장 적절합니다.

④: 직접 관찰보다 기억에 의존해야 한다는 주장은 본문의 '관찰의 중요성'과 상반되므로 오답입니다.

⑤: 추상화에서 원근법이 덜 중요하다는 내용은 지문에서 다루지 않고 있으며, 지문의 논리 흐름과 맞지 않습니다.

13) ③

해설

①: 높은 수요와 경제 활동은 지문에서 문제로 언급된 '공급 축

소로 인한 유가 상승'과는 다른 원인입니다.

②: 에너지 기업의 수익 증가가 본문에서 언급되었지만, 그 자체가 중심 논지를 뒷받침하는 문장은 아닙니다.

③: 'A look through the history of oil price fluctuations proves this notion'이라는 문장은 다음 문단에 실제로 등장하며, 유가 상승이 경제에 미치는 부정적 영향을 구체적인 예로 설명하기에 가장 적절한 연결 문장입니다.

④: 정부의 개입은 지문에 언급되지 않았습니다.

⑤: 소비자 혜택에 대한 설명은 문단의 주제인 거시경제적 영향과는 방향이 다릅니다.

14) ②
해설

①: 교육 환경에서 자아 인식이 방해된다는 내용은 지문과 무관합니다.

②: 'The most effective communicators find ways to make the abstract personal'이라는 문장은 정보가 자기와 연관될수록 더 효과적으로 전달된다는 지문 핵심 내용을 직접 나타내므로 가장 적절한 선택입니다.

③: 믿음을 지지하지 않는 정보 무시는 본문에서 다룬 바 없습니다.

④: 구체적 표현이 일반적 진술보다 덜 설득력 있다는 주장은 지문 사례("Look to your left…")와 반대입니다.

⑤: 집단 정체성보다는 개인적 관련성, 즉 'self'가 핵심이므로 오답입니다.

15) ③
해설

①: 디지털 도구를 단순화한다는 표현은 지문 흐름과 맞지 않습니다.

②: 사무실 구조의 모방은 지문에서 직접 언급된 표현이 아닙니다.

③: 지문 내 "Steve Jobs understood that using familiar terms would make the new technology easier to understand."라는 문장을 그대로 반영한 내용으로, 빈칸에 가장 적절한 정답입니다.

④: 파일 관리 속도를 개선한다는 내용은 지문에서 다뤄지지 않았습니다.

⑤: 기술 용어를 피하는 것보다, 익숙한 용어를 활용하는 점이 본문의 핵심입니다.

16) ②
해설

①: 오늘날 환경에서도 여전히 잘 작동한다는 내용은 지문의 핵심 주장과 상반됩니다. 지문에서는 이러한 단서들이 현재에는 오히려 위험하게 작용한다고 설명하고 있습니다.

②: "Turtles are basing their decisions on simple cues that were perfectly rational for their ancestors"라는 문장은 지문에 그대로 제시되어 있으며, 과거에는 합리적이었으나

현대에는 문제가 되는 단서라는 주장을 잘 보여주는 정답입니다.

③: 최근 과학적 발견에 대한 언급은 지문에 없습니다.

④: 단서가 세대마다 무작위로 선택된다는 주장은 진화적 설명과 모순되므로 부적절합니다.

⑤: '단순한 단서(simple cues)'라는 표현과 어긋나므로 오답입니다.

17) ②
해설

①: 감각을 무시해도 된다는 주장은 본문 내용과 정반대입니다.

②: 지문의 마지막 문장 "we need constant input from our senses to carry out functions that give us personality and intellect."을 그대로 반영한 문장으로, 빈칸에 가장 적절한 정답입니다.

③: 자극 없이 작동한다는 주장은 본문 "the brain is not designed to sense on its own"과 모순됩니다.

④: 환각이 수면 중에만 발생한다는 내용은 지문에 없으며, 오답입니다.

⑤: 감각 차단이 사고를 명확하게 만든다는 주장 역시 지문 실험 결과와 반대되므로 오답입니다.

18) ③
해설

①: 자동 반응이 현대 실험으로 처음 발견되었다는 언급은 지문에 없습니다.

②: 고도의 스트레스 상황에서도 의식적으로 통제된다는 내용은 지문과 상반됩니다. 지문에서는 무의식적 반응이 강조됩니다.

③: 'our feet communicate exactly what we think and feel more honestly…'라는 문장은 지문 도입부에서 이미 언급된 핵심 내용이며, 바로 앞 문장의 설명을 자연스럽게 이어주는 문장으로 빈칸에 적절합니다.

④: 문화적으로 학습된 행동이라는 주장은 본문의 '진화적 본능 반응'이라는 핵심과 반대되므로 오답입니다.

⑤: 무의식적 반응이 진화적으로 억제되었다는 주장도 본문 내용과 맞지 않습니다.

19) ③
해설

①: 예술적 장식 가능성은 지문의 주요 논지인 '자료 보존성과 실용성'과 관련이 없어 오답입니다.

②: 구술 전통의 완전한 폐지는 지문에서 언급되지 않았으며 과도한 추론입니다.

③: 로마인이 두루마리를 책(codex) 형식으로 바꾼 것이 종이의 잠재력을 최대한 끌어냈다고 설명하는 문맥에서, 책 형식이 정보를 더 쉽게 접근하고 보존할 수 있게 했다는 이 문장이 가장 자연스럽고 핵심 내용을 잘 반영한 정답입니다.

④: 두루마리의 장식성과 의례적 가치에 대한 언급은 지문에

없습니다.
⑤: 정치적 갈등으로 초기 책이 소실되었다는 내용도 본문과 무관합니다.

20) ③
해설
①: 경제 전문가에게 맡겨야 한다는 주장은 지문 흐름과 맞지 않습니다.
②: 널리 받아들여진 사실에 근거한다는 말은 지문에서 강조하는 '논리적 전개 필요성'과 거리가 있습니다.
③: 다양한 아이디어들이 복합적으로 얽혀 있음을 설명한 문장 뒤에, "따라서 우리는 그 이유를 구성 요소로 나누어 분석해야 한다"는 이 문장은 자연스럽고 핵심 논지를 정확히 반영한 정답입니다.
④: 설득력보다 논리적 정당화가 지문의 초점이므로 오답입니다.
⑤: 직관적 연결에 의존해서는 안 된다는 것이 지문 전체의 요지이므로 오답입니다.

21) ③
해설
①: 정치적 논의에서 드물게 언급된다는 내용은 지문에 없습니다.
②: 언론이 문제를 과장한다는 내용은 일부 타당해 보일 수 있으나, 본문의 핵심은 이분법적 사고를 벗어나 이주가 '해결책이 될 수 있음'을 강조하는 점에 있습니다.
③: "migration can also be a solution for many preexisting problems"라는 문장은 다음 문장 ("out-migration generally redistributes workers…")과 논리적으로 자연스럽게 이어지며, 지문 전체의 주장을 정확히 반영한 정답입니다.
④: 지문에서 이주자는 대체로 젊고 유연하며 회복력이 있다는 점을 강조하고 있습니다.
⑤: 정부의 제한 조치는 언급되지 않았습니다.

22) ④
해설
①: 정부에 대한 신뢰 확보가 직접적으로 언급되진 않으며, 본문의 초점은 '통화량 제한'에 있습니다.
②: 자유로운 대출은 지문과 관련이 없습니다. 오히려 제한적인 통화 공급과는 반대 개념입니다.
③: 금을 기준으로 한 시스템은 오히려 종이 화폐의 금 교환을 허용하므로 오답입니다.
④: 제한된 자원을 화폐로 사용함으로써 정부가 통화를 무제한으로 찍어내는 것을 방지한다는 문맥과 정확히 일치하는 설명으로, 빈칸에 가장 적절한 문장입니다.
⑤: 정부가 금의 가치를 조작할 수 있다는 내용은 지문과 상반되며, 오답입니다.

23) ③

해설
①: 현대 신경과학에서 널리 받아들여진다는 말은 일부 사실일 수 있지만, 바로 이어지는 문장에서 'conventional economics'와 대비되는 내용을 다루므로 흐름상 적절하지 않습니다.
②: 전통적 경제학에서 확인된 것이 아니라, 오히려 그것과 반대되는 결과이므로 오답입니다.
③: 감정이 결정에 긍정적 역할을 한다는 주장은 기존 경제학 이론의 '비감정적이고 최적화된 결정' 전제와 반대되므로, "This finding stands in sharp contrast to traditional economic theory"라는 문장이 논리적으로 자연스럽게 이어집니다.
④: 감정이 해롭다는 주장 역시 지문과 상반되므로 오답입니다.
⑤: 논리만으로 최적 선택이 이루어진다는 관점은 기존 경제학의 주장에 해당하며, 지문의 핵심 주장과는 반대입니다.

24) ④
해설
①: 더 나은 선택지에 대한 인식을 제한한다는 내용은 본문과 맞지 않습니다.
②: 각각의 단점을 무시한다는 말은, 실제로는 단점을 인식하고 후회한다는 지문과 반대됩니다.
③: 결정으로부터 감정적으로 멀어진다는 말은 지문 맥락과 어울리지 않습니다.
④: "This both increases our fear of making the wrong choice and raises expectations…"라는 문장을 그대로 반영한 것으로, 지문과 정확히 일치하므로 정답입니다.
⑤: 혜택을 깨닫지 못한다는 내용은 지문의 핵심 주장에서 벗어납니다.

25) ④
해설
①: 망설임이 행동을 멈춰야 한다는 신호라는 해석은 본문의 결말과 어긋납니다.
②: 다른 사람이 도와주기를 기다리는 것이 좋다는 주장은 지문의 메시지와 반대입니다.
③: 돕는 것이 오히려 상황을 악화시킨다는 내용도 본문의 따뜻한 결말과 일치하지 않습니다.
④: 마지막 문장 "even the smallest act of help is much better for someone in need than doing nothing"은 Linda의 깨달음을 그대로 나타내며, 지문을 마무리하는 데 가장 적절한 정답입니다.
⑤: 곤란한 상황에서 도움을 고마워하지 않는다는 주장은 지문 속 미소와 감사 표현과 모순됩니다.

Quiz 4 **Answers**

1. thank
2. commitment
3. boosted

4. draws
5. close
6. reviewing
7. influence
8. extend
9. another
10. efforts
11. enrich
12. educational
13. hearing
14. icy
15. carrying
16. flushed
17. worse
18. appeared
19. refused
20. drop
21. reception
22. worry
23. thoroughly
24. injection
25. ease
26. sense
27. relief
28. finest
29. placing
30. water
31. brew
32. function
33. allowing
34. interact
35. flourish
36. barriers
37. distance
38. connect
39. around
40. blend
41. collaborate
42. engage
43. within
44. broader
45. set
46. control
47. fixed
48. anyone
49. Satisfaction
50. depending
51. balance
52. possess
53. solely
54. without
55. expectations
56. meaningless
57. define
58. miss
59. content
60. vastly
61. wealth
62. lack
63. long
64. personal
65. adjust
66. attainable
67. select
68. dishes
69. tempting
70. attract
71. version
72. rely
73. patrons
74. lure
75. catchy
76. promote
77. various
78. glowing
79. flowers
80. scent

81. prefer
82. choose
83. amount
84. earn
85. return
86. decision
87. added
88. makes
89. up
90. delay
91. associated
92. rather
93. immediately
94. scenarios
95. waiting
96. yield
97. extra
98. logical
99. immediacy
100. refer
101. present
102. sacrifice
103. obtain
104. sooner
105. key
106. exactly
107. identified
108. begin
109. belief
110. indicates
111. reach
112. age
113. cases
114. revealed
115. appears
116. scans
117. fetuses
118. exhibited
119. percentage
120. quite
121. roughly
122. individuals
123. population
124. illustrates
125. Of
126. volume
127. throughout
128. period
129. declined
130. whereas
131. increases
132. timeframe
133. double
134. growth
135. increase
136. during
137. decreased
138. regarded
139. displayed
140. initially
141. turning
142. ruins
143. architecture
144. project
145. considered
146. notable
147. enhanced
148. achievement
149. magnificent
150. invented
151. performances
152. laid
153. rest
154. develop
155. enhance
156. welcoming
157. Information:

158. exclusively	235. engages
159. covers	236. sense
160. airfare	237. self
161. details	238. adopt
162. Protect	239. place
163. Location	240. environment
164. free	241. tangible
165. charge	242. operating
166. litter	243. unfamiliar
167. case	244. alike
168. free	245. transition
169. several	246. public
170. techniques	247. parallels
171. varying	248. well-known
172. rules	249. digital
173. convey	250. placed
174. essential	251. adopted
175. possess	252. everyday
176. reality	253. language
177. observe	254. grasp
178. translate	255. similarities
179. aim	256. office
180. reflect	257. appear
181. look	258. instinct
182. depending	259. sense
183. viewpoint	260. meant
184. crucial	261. ocean's
185. consistent	262. guided
186. angle	263. arose
187. maintain	264. constructing
188. throughout	265. lit
189. perceive	266. newly
190. capturing	267. drawn
191. appearance	268. head
192. practicing	269. dangerous
193. beneficial	270. rely
194. reduced	271. served
195. sectors	272. Unfortunately,
196. automotive	273. modern
197. gain	274. reliable
198. lower	275. disrupted
199. turn	276. artificial
200. promotes	277. means
201. increase	278. interacting
202. rarely	279. perceive
203. significantly	280. itself
204. benefit	281. detect
205. widely	282. contact
206. rise	283. identify
207. constraints	284. areas
208. experience	285. principle
209. slowdown	286. demonstrated
210. translates	287. immersed
211. output	288. sensory
212. declining	289. disorganized
213. oversupply	290. continuous
214. rarely	291. essential
215. economic	292. maintaining
216. story	293. processes
217. already	294. reveal
218. memorable	295. emotions
219. easily	296. indicators
220. accessible	297. feel
221. centered	298. advent
222. spent	299. instinctively
223. ourselves	300. responded
224. dominated	301. aggressive
225. relates	302. requiring
226. process	303. ensured
227. deeply	304. appropriately
228. resonates	305. stopping
229. never	306. fleeing
230. Skilled	307. dangers
231. abstract	308. mechanism
232. highlighting	309. passed
233. challenges	310. effective
234. impersonal	311. remains

312. ancient
313. ingrained
314. encounter
315. discomfort
316. shift
317. hands-on
318. culture
319. text
320. delayed
321. practical
322. Early
323. fragile
324. difficult
325. prone
326. immobile
327. available
328. addressed
329. issues
330. written
331. innovation
332. remains
333. communication
334. relatively
335. ultimately
336. primary
337. medium
338. preserving
339. rarely
340. statement
341. summarize
342. briefly
343. interplay
344. understand
345. series
346. stating
347. come
348. sentence
349. concerns
350. brings
351. concepts
352. connection
353. goal
354. taking
355. granted
356. examine
357. clarify
358. relationships
359. elements
360. portrayed
361. strain
362. contribute
363. belief
364. driven
365. crises
366. pursuing
367. indeed
368. challenges
369. address
370. moves
371. regions
372. tend
373. adaptable
374. difficulties
375. pursuit
376. improved
377. compared
378. home
379. impacts
380. across
381. migrants'
382. new
383. issued
384. power
385. additional
386. repeated
387. resulting
388. come

389. counter
390. naturally
391. approach
392. restrict
393. excessively
394. choice
395. quickly
396. exchanged
397. holder
398. referred
399. assumes
400. directly
401. value
402. function
403. impose
404. interest
405. utilizing
406. individuals
407. impairments
408. regions
409. associated
410. affect
411. areas
412. diminishes
413. quality
414. working
415. challenges
416. traditional
417. detrimental
418. sound
419. conventional
420. detached
421. rational
422. vital
423. faced
424. purchase
425. offered
426. six
427. individually
428. decreases
429. regardless
430. select
431. difficulty
432. compels
433. drawbacks
434. lament
435. absence
436. phenomenon
437. enhancing
438. abundance
439. hampers
440. heighten
441. anxious
442. overwhelmed
443. option
444. choice
445. arrived
446. murmur
447. eager
448. boarding
449. settling
450. beside
451. far
452. frame
453. welcome
454. offer
455. act
456. moment
457. regaining
458. conscious
459. calmed
460. returned
461. steadier
462. passing
463. reflected
464. offering
465. kindness

466. standing

1. A school appreciates a teacher's excellent work and offers to renew her contract.

2. A father takes his sick daughter to the hospital and feels relieved after treatment.

3. Just as tea needs water, people need connection because leaders must not isolate themselves from others.

4. Desire for wealth is endless because happiness depends on expectations, not just possessions.

5. Flowers attract pollinators using scent, much like restaurants use vivid words to attract customers.

6. People often choose smaller rewards now over larger ones later due to emotional decision-making.

7. Right-handedness often begins before birth, as shown in studies using fetal arm movement.

8. Mexico led U.S. dairy imports, but Indonesia showed the fastest growth from 2018 to 2020.

9. Brunelleschi, a Renaissance architect, created many masterpieces and revolutionized building design.

10. Youth Leaders Camp develops leadership through teamwork, cultural tours, and project presentations in Canada.

11. Join an eco-friendly event to jog, pick up trash, and help the Earth at Lake Union.

12. Artists use perspective techniques to draw realistic, three-dimensional images on flat surfaces.

13. Oil price drops help most industries grow, while rises reduce economic output and growth.

14. We remember information better when it connects to ourselves, making personal relevance powerful.

15. Steve Jobs used everyday analogies to help people accept and understand new computer technology.

16. Turtles evolved to follow light to the sea, but human lights now misguide them dangerously.

17. Our brain depends entirely on senses to function and understand the outside world clearly.

18. Feet reflect honest emotions because they evolved to react instantly to danger for survival.

19. Paper replaced heavy materials in writing, helping written culture spread through the invention of books.

20. Strong arguments require breaking down broad reasons into specific, logical supporting ideas.

21. Migration, often seen as a crisis, also offers solutions by redistributing labor and opportunity.

22. Limiting money supply with gold prevents inflation caused by governments printing excess money.

23. Emotions help us make better decisions, contrary to the belief that logic alone is best.

24. Too many choices make people unhappy by increasing regret and fear of making wrong decisions.

25. Linda helps a fainting woman on a train, learning small kindnesses matter in uncertain moments.

Quiz 5 **Answers**

1) improving
2) contract
3) calmness
4) peacefully
5) water
6) isolated
7) relative
8) expects
9) attract
10) advertisement
11) hyperbolic
12) inconsistent
13) Handedness
14) fertilization
15) imports
16) country
17) architecture
18) ancient
19) leadership
20) planning
21) Plogging
22) conserve
23) viewpoint
24) dimensional
25) costs
26) energy
27) connections
28) abstract
29) analogies
30) virtual
31) hatchlings
32) evolved
33) sensory
34) mind
35) threats

36) hardwired
37) literate
38) written
39) complex
40) assumed
41) labor
42) destination
43) inflation
44) governments
45) negative
46) neuroscience
47) regret
48) tyranny
49) elderly
50) hesitation
51) improved
52) extension
53) continued
54) fever
55) peacefully
56) calm
57) contact
58) leaders
59) isolation
60) no
61) expectations
62) horizon
63) attract
64) words
65) advertise
66) immediate
67) hyperbolic
68) discounting
69) emotional
70) inconsistent
71) before
72) ultrasound
73) right
74) dairy
75) increases
76) drop
77) smaller
78) Roman
79) architect
80) machinery
81) leadership
82) culture
83) project
84) Plogging
85) Free
86) provided
87) depth
88) perspective
89) viewpoint
90) three
91) lower
92) costs
93) boost
94) reduced
95) excess
96)
97) abstract
98) personal
99) relatable
100) analogy
101) virtual
102) familiar
103) understand
104) hatchlings
105) rational
106) decision
107) cannot
108) sensory
109) constant
110) honestly
111) reflect
112) without

113) hardwired
114) oral
115) literate
116) poor
117) dominant
118) complex
119) precise
120) avoiding
121) Migration
122) opportunity
123) labor
124) destination
125) inflation
126) limited
127) limiting
128) emotions
129) decision
130) deliberative
131) challenging
132) reduce
133) tyranny
134) lacks
135) elderly
136) hesitation
137) urgent

내신 완벽 대비
변형 문제집 **잉글리쉬 마이갓**

변형 문제 더 보기